Exposing the Expositions:
Ancient Rome in America?

by

Howdie Mickoski

Cataloging in Publication Data:
ISBN
978-82-691266-1-7

Cover design by: Ladyjaska
Cover Photo: CD Arnold 1893, special collections Chicago Public Library

TABLE OF CONTENTS

"*In a time of universal deceit, telling the truth becomes a revolutionary act.*"

George Orwell, 1984

PREFACE
What is this book?

"Every record has been destroyed or falsified, every book rewritten, every picture has been repainted, every statue and street building has been renamed, every date has been altered. And the process is continuing day by day and minute by minute. History has stopped. Nothing exists except and endless present in which the party is always right." George Orwell, 1984

I have been asked by several people "why did I write such a controversial book? In fact a book where deep questions seem to have no concrete answers until we have access to a time machine. There is really nothing for me to "gain" by doing so. Most people will not buy such a book- so it has not been for money. I have given up eight months of my life to study and write it, time that could have gone to other pursuits. So it has not been for saving time. Many of those that do in fact read it (or even just hear about it) will think I have gone a bit loopy to be researching such a topic. So is not for standing in the community that I have done this. I have also been mostly alone in this project, a lonely yet equally satisfying period to produce this. So why did I write and publish it?

I feel that I was almost forced to write it. Days after returning from a week in Florence, and filled with the energy of Renaissance masterpieces, the strange history of the Expositions came into my field of vision. They had to be examined, and as yet, no one really had. There has been a few Youtube videos and some blog posts, but no one took the time to write an entire book on the idea that these giant Expos might have been something entirely different than standard history presents. So part of my need to continue this project was to get something available for the population to read (for those who still value a book over something they watch on a screen) and as a way to inspire others in this field doing research on similar topics that they too should put their findings to print.

Some today like to present that George Orwell's novel *1984* is now becoming our reality. They point to various elements of the control and monitoring of the population that is occurring. What they miss is the main element that Orwell claimed was needed as the foundation for it all. If you want to control a population, you first have to control history. A main piece of his novel is about how The Party has, and was still, rewriting history in order to serve its own needs.

I am writing this with the hope that you my friend, will take time to think about the history you have been presented in schools, books and documentaries. How can you know if it is true? How much is being taken on face value that "the experts" know what they are talking about? What evidence are the experts using to prove their own theories? Don't agree with me just because I am writing something in this book, likewise don't continue to believe what you have always believed, just because you liked Mr. Jenkins in 11th grade history class or that swanky new History Channel program. Use this book as a call to think for yourself. Open up the entire field of history fresh, and ask, really ask for the first time- what actually is true?

Please note, that unlike my previous books, I did not have the resources to pay for a professional edit of this material beyond chapter three. I have done the best that I can...but some errors will remain in this text. Please appreciate the challenge it is for me to get this in book form. A lonely endeavor can mean some lone errors can remain.

I want to state clearly that I do not have the answer as to what really happened in our history. We are but some 60 years past the JFK assassination and the moon landings, and we are still not really sure what is true or not true with those events. The further we go back in the past, the less sure we are about everything. All we can do is to start with the examination of standard history as it is presented, and openly ask- What is the proof that is provided for any historical "fact." Doing so most "historical facts" become seen to be as nothing more than a story. And like all stories, they tell more about the author than the story itself.

As you will soon see by reading this book, the foundation of all we have come to know as our modern world seems to have its origin in the mid to late 1800's...right at the time Giant Expositions are being built and then destroyed. They may be like a photographic window to a now "covered over" history.

CHAPTER 1
THE PROBLEM

Chicago 1893, Court of Honor

"What the hell, that's insane," I mutter this to myself as I look at a series of images on my computer screen. One of those images is directly above this text, a photo labeled "Court of Honor." You would think one might be looking at a recreation of Ancient Rome, or at least a photo of some Central European city like Vienna or Budapest around one hundred years ago. The time period is correct, but not the location. No, we are looking at a photograph of the 1893 Chicago World's Fair. Held just twenty years after the city was burned down by the Great Fire of 1871, they built on a massive scale to hold the 1893 Exposition. Look at the area, and the other photos in upcoming chapters. Colossal buildings (one could hold 300,000 people), giant domes, towers, and colonnade pillars. All on a site almost 700 acres. That is 2.8 square kilometers. The Exposition included buildings for every state, every country, a giant midway area, lakes, lagoons, and everything with fine ornamentation and artwork. This was all claimed to be built, from scratch, in less than two years. Then as soon as it ended, they tore it all down throwing the remains of all the buildings into landfills. Hence the reason I muttered, "That's insane."

Originally I thought this was going to be a one or two month project on the Chicago Fair, discussing the oddities of it, and making a few hypotheses. But that turned into months of detailed research because it was not just Chicago where this insanity happened. Similar World Expositions occurred in New York, Philadelphia, Buffalo, St Louis and San Francisco (just nine years after their earthquake). Louisville, Omaha, Nashville and New Orleans all built massive buildings for their regional fairs. There were fairs in Paris, London, Barcelona, Melbourne, Lima, Copenhagen, Brussels, Cambodia- just about everywhere in the world. All with magnificent "supposedly" temporary structures, and then having all of the buildings torn down right afterwards. Why build such magnificent structures then just destroy them? So I began looking into it...and a lot of things just do not add up; including the time frames considered for building these structures. Even to the history of the exposition cities themselves. Just about everything in the history of the world between 1800-1920 seems incredibly strange once you begin to examine it. At the center point of the strangeness appears to be these World Fairs, acting like a lighthouse saying 'look here.'

World Exhibitions (or Fairs in the US), started in 1851 in London and were supposed to have became a focus for nations to show off their new found industrial and scientific "progress" being made, while also presenting cultural concepts to reveal Social Darwinism (people today are better than those in the past, industrial people are better than primitive people). It was the new elite that financed the expositions, and who were its main attendees. World Fairs inspired all the modern amusement parks and even theme parks like Disneyland. But there was so much more to these 19th century fairs than amusement. They were called Expositions for a reason.

Twenty years ago I was introduced to the understanding that the ancient world, (Egypt, Mexico, Peru etc) was not anything like the archaeologists were telling us. That the pyramids, cut granite stones and statues were beyond what we could construct or create today. It was inspiring to say the least, the possibility that ancient civilization was so far beyond our own in terms of technology, wisdom and understanding- that I in a sense gave up my normal life and spent 10 years to travel, research and write a 500 page book called *The Power Of Then*. While I had known much of what we call modern history was not totally truthful, it has only been recently that it has come to be seen as just as big a lie as what I had examined in Egypt and Mexico. A great civilization might have existed into the 1800's, one that has been systematically eliminated from history. It survives today in pieces that few can recognize. that seemed to be destroyed by a powerful cataclysm or warfare with technology not supposed to exist. While all of this can be hard for anyone to take in, at times it has been very hard for me personally.

You see I have my degree in history. Finished with excellent grades, wrote papers, thesis, even at times argued with professors on subjects. Thought I might even become a professor as well and live the good life behind the ivy walls. But never at the time did I ever think that the basic foundation of all we call history, is just a story- "his" story.[1]. That my time at university was actually indoctrinating me even more. University was supposed to try to teach me to think critically, yet only within the box of the standard (stones were pulled on ropes to build pyramids, battles happened when and how it says in the books, gladiators fought in the Colosseum, that North America were only populated by native peoples before the 1600's). But within those boxes it did teach me to think about the bias of an author or researcher. A book about Stalingrad in 1942 would be written very differently by a Soviet writer from a German writer. So one has to learn to read through the author's ideas and beliefs to see what the base research reveals. This has served me well, and it is this background that I feel gives me an advantage to delve into the mass of material this book series is going to look at.

I want you too to read this book critically, don't just accept what is here. Think about it. Look up source materials, do some reading yourself. I can do my best to present why I believe the standard story can not be close to correct, and some directions to walk to for what could then be true. Answers in this field (without a time machine) are nearly impossible to get. What we can do though is examine the standard historical story with great critical detail. What of it can be proven, 100% proven. You will see very little. Most of it can not even

---

[1]

Who is the "his" that the world history is referring to? Mostly it is thought to refer to men, as in men made all the wars,were the kings so they wrote the history. There is partial truth in that, but I believe the his being referred to in this context might in fact be a direct reference to someone, or something very specific! See chapter 8.

have a 20% proof rate. It thus demands a direct open-minded investigation. People have to look at the past, and really think about it.

"*People do not like to think. If one really thinks, one must reach conclusions. Conclusions are not always pleasant.*" Helen Keller, who gave a lecture at the 1904 St Louis Exposition

History is one of the most important subjects to study and understand, and it the MOST likely to be disliked by students (for it is taught in a boring manner of the memorization of dates and names). The subject is thought of as useless. But history is incredibly important, because as George Orwell reminded us in his book *1984* "He who controls the present, controls the future. He who controls the past, controls the present." Everything we do, are and believe is somehow rooted in the past (either our personal past of events) or as a collective (the past we call world history). It tells us who we are as a species, and why were are like the way we are now. But it is very clear on just a little study that all history is only a hypotheses. Very little can be verified. This is not the presentation students get today, where they are told the textbook is right, memorize it, say it on the test, pass-then you never have to think of it again. But if you don't fully examine and dig through history to find the lies, it is not that you will be condemned to repeat it, but far worse. You will be condemned to live the very existence that lie creates. It is our presented history that creates the current bondage, destruction, suffering and lack. But what if the history of this place is something totally different? The story of these expositions is totally different.

It can be quite a ride to honestly study history, but it can also be very disturbing for the foundation of the self that is directly linked to it. To uncover any lies of history will be to uncover a piece of the lie of the self. It is why the resistance for many is so strong to study these topics. You are not just taking apart the history in a book, you are taking apart yourself, one lie at a time. In my book *Falling For Truth,* I wrote of how we use a false (or at least unproven) point-of-reference for how we view ourselves and reality. Part of that point-of-reference is what we call history.

View from the Electrical Tower, St Louis Exhibition 1904

This book will look at World Exhibitions held between 1850-1915. Seems like a simple thing right? City holds a big fair, constructs a bunch of buildings, presents a ton of technology and "progress." Millions come to the city. Sort of like an Olympics of showing off. We still have them. Montreal in 1967 and Vancouver in 2010 recently for those of us who are Canadian. Food, beer, midway rides, an art gallery, a new car exhibit, a funky space age building. Voila, fair. But as you see in the above photo, the fairs of hundred years ago are nothing like what they have become. The Australian World Exposition Project Sponsors Report in 1966 claimed that "of all the events of recent history, only wars have had a more dramatic influence than World Expositions upon the expression of civilization."[2] We are not just looking at history, we will be looking at how history was being invented and presented, sent to the world's population through the fairs.

What is odd is that every World Expo city prior to 1915 had a giant fire in its recent past. In Chicago's case just 20 years prior to the Exposition. Then the buildings was just torn down. You can sense the question that I have immediately. If a city that has just lost most of its buildings in a massive fire, why would they immediately tear down some giant buildings that were just put up? That led me wonder not only how fast the fairs were supposed built, but how fast the cities themselves

---

[2] Found in the Arthur Chandler essay *L Exposition publique Paris 1798*

were built. In times that seem impossible even with modern building machinery.

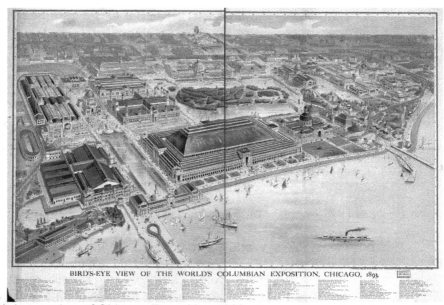
BIRD'S-EYE VIEW OF THE WORLD'S COLUMBIAN EXPOSITION, CHICAGO, 1893

Birds eye view of Chicago Exposition 1893

The image above is the Chicago Exposition, all 700 acres of it, and all suggested to have been magically built in less than two years. The same story is presented for the 1,200 acre exposition in St. Louis of 1904. The historical claim for what ALL THAT could be built in two years was due to it having been all constructed out of temporary materials. But is that true? Did they really build all temporary buildings, and in the time frame specified? I asked a number of building contractors to get their input, and they claimed very clearly that the time frames given for the building of these expositions was just not possible. These are not theorists, they construct buildings every day of their life, and even given a modern machine-equipped workforce, they were clear the time frame for the building was not possible. No matter what the material was being used, to do that in two years to them is just not possible. The best time frame they could give me, with modern machines, was 15 years. I will go into detail of exactly why they say this in upcoming chapters.

The usual response from the historian of how this was achieved is "old world craftsmanship." OK. but if you are a craftsman in your work, while you produce something terrific, it should take LONGER not shorter

12

to build. These expositions are record building, with incredible finish and ornamentation that would rival what is witnessed in Ancient Rome. And how were they hauling the materials to the site? Digging and landscaping acres of land? Feeding and supplying the work force? The more you study the structures, the more amazing it all becomes. It will not take long, especially with the commentary of the building contractors, to show that the "story" of the building of these fairs in two years are giant lies. The question becomes, what then could be the truth?

I see there are three likely scenarios.[3] The first could be that the exposition constructions really took 30 or 40 years to build, and for some reason was lied about to be a few years. The history books are clear the Chicago Fair only got the go ahead in 1890, and began planing and landscaping in 1891, and since I do not think the Chicago Expo was being built in 1851 the same time as London, we must move to the next theory. The second, more likely scenario, is that the construction did take only two years to complete, but for that to be true it would mean the builders in the 1890's had access to a highly advanced technology for building and transportation that they were not supposed to have. Some have suggested some type of 3-d printing, where the entire thing could be generated on site, even perhaps ordered as if from a kit. Another suggestion is that they builders had a direct access to free electrical energy that was used to operate electrical machines as we have today. The Chicago expo had an above ground electric railroad, and you could ride the harbor in electric boats. Where all this electricity was coming from in 1893, and what happened to these boats and trains is never answered. This is a theory that could hold weight.

The third theory is that many of the buildings had been there for hundreds, perhaps even a thousand years. That they were products of a much older civilization, possibly buried in various catastrophes perhaps not that far into the past, now labeled under the catch all term mudflood. As such the buildings were not built, but dug out, (or perhaps there was no need to dig them out, they were simply there aged and weathered). Thus they did not need to be built- but refurbished and painted to look new. This is something that could possibly fit a two or three year time line, while constructing some temporary (similar looking buildings along side) to confuse anyone into what was new and what was old. Could some of the buildings at these expositions have already been there long

---

[3] Of course there are many others, including magic, building them in parallel universes, having aliens come in their spaceships to build them. Here though, I will stick with the three most likely to me at this point.

before the supposed construction process began? If either of these final two hypothesis are even close to true it would change history drastically.

Just who built New York's original Pennsylvania Station, shown here in 1910?

On further examination, every city in US since 1800 was constructing spectacular buildings (such as the photos above like New York's original Penn Station or Washington's Old Post Office). Most were also torn down within 50 years (while looking weathered like they were 2-300 year old buildings) or burned in strange fires (such as all the Crystal Palaces around the world). A few of these spectacular buildings still stand today as universities, cathedrals, libraries, art galleries, hotels or simply as homes for the rich. The same is true for South America and Australia (where convicts jump off a boat then within twenty years have Cathedrals to rival France). Perhaps the first "Europeans" to the Americas and Australia did not build the great cities of these continents, they found them already there?

That is why this examination of this period of time is so important. Trying to understand what the evidence of the surviving buildings, and what the thousands of photographs from the 1800's tell us. Perhaps the towers, domes, star forts and colossal architecture were not just things to look nice, but were designed originally to create free electrical (even healing) energy to the city or area. Perhaps our mechanized, technological world is not the top of Darwin's pyramid, we

14

might be nothing but the mud pit of history. A mud pit that might have a literal truth in the past on the ground. And the World Expositions might be the missing link in the puzzle that can help us answer what really happened in our past.

I am not going to examine all the detail of these exhibitions for that would be a monumental undertaking (a 9-volume set of books from St Louis Exposition of 1904 is about 4,000 pages). I have listed these sources in the Bibliography so you can look into more detail if you wish. Instead in this book I want to focus on the story of how and why these buildings were constructed, as well as some of the underlying principles of Social Darwinism expressed in the fairs. Fairs in which each one made you believe you were in Ancient Rome, which I do not feel was a co-incidence or by accident.

New words will be presented in the text like mudflood (cities seemingly have been partially covered in mud sometime in the last 200 years, but can also refer to any disaster to hit a city between the years 1600-1900), reset (the idea that these city disasters were not accidental by nature, but were somehow orchestrated by an external force), free energy (the use of these buildings to create energy either for electricity or healing based on the building's domes, towers, copper, mercury, type of stone and the shape), or alternative history (change to the standard historical narrative)[4].

To overcome the lie of history takes years of digging (no pun intended), and this work is just the beginning, but I feel it is an important beginning nonetheless.

---

[4] now often associated with a Russian mathematician Anatoly Fomenko who is widely followed but of whom I have some concerns with.

CHAPTER 2
WORLD FAIR ORIGINS

"The first step in liquidating a people is to erase its memory. Destroy its books, its culture, its history. Then have somebody write new books, manufacture a new culture, invent a new history. Before long that nation will begin to forget what it is and what it was. The world around it will forget even faster" Milan Kundera, The Book of Laughter and Forgetting

Mechanical Building, Chicago 1893

World's Expositions are now "sanctioned" by the Bureau International des Expositions (BIE) in Paris. Their website has a listing of all major world expos, as well as a few photos of many of them. But to really examine them one must expand the research investigation. The studylove site of John Paul Sanks (studylove.org/worldsfairs) is a great source for finding much out there available on these events, with links to original photographs, articles and books. An interesting source for Chicago I have come across is *The Book of The Fair*, by Hubert Howe Bancroft.[5] It is 1500 pages of information, and was published in 1895 just after the Exposition concluded, so as to provide the message of the

---

[5] It is found for free online at columbus dot lit dot edu.

times. I will examine Bancroft later for he is as much a part of the writing as the writing itself. Each of the major expositions had their own historian to write a massive document of not just of the event itself, but the entire world history leading up to them. It is almost to me as in the Kundera quote above, these historical books are not so much presenting history as presenting the history that those in command want everyone to believe.

Bancroft begins his book with a long examination of commerce and trade in Egypt, but specifically Phoenicia, and claims these gatherings were always held as **sacred places** (my emphasis), and of how the Ancient Greeks held adjoining fairs for the Olympics and at Delphi. When it comes to fairs thousands of yeas in the past he describes, "In the majority of instances the ancient fairs were established in connection with religious festivals, and hence were held within or near **some place of worship, or on some sacred spot, as around the shrine of a martyr, or the tomb of a saint**. At first these gatherings were purely for devotional purposes, but presently a certain business was transacted in provisions, the demand for which increased with the influx of worshipers. Then came the idea of profiting by this traffic, followed by the attendance of merchants who offered for sale a variety of wares." In 1893 the organizers wanted to lay claim that the current Exhibitions were somehow direct descendants of the ancient world.

The underlying message being presented was that ancient fairs were held at sacred spots. So should the place that the expositions occurred in Philadelphia, New York, Chicago, or Paris be thought of as sacred spots? Not because a fair took place there, but because they were already sacred somehow prior, and that is why the fair was placed there.

Basic history claims that what became the modern Great Fairs evolved from local English and French Fairs of the 1700's, which were a sort of combined business exhibit and public entertainment for the local area. His look at French fairs are very telling, for after mentioning the fairs at Lyons and St Denis (granted to the monks by Dagobert), he then mentions two locations- Champagne and Troys. These are the two French sites that are most connected with the stories of the Holy Grail and with the Knights Templar (whose charter came at Troys). This is an interesting thing to consider, the early French fairs are linked with the two most mysterious concepts of the last 1000 years.

17

While the first overly large fair happened at the end of the 1700's in Prague, as part of the coronation of Leopold II as king of Bohemia in 1797, it was an Exhibition the next year 1798 in Paris that was special. Current history still claims that the first World "sanctioned" fair happened in England in 1851 as mentioned. But this is untrue. "The first one worthy of the name, though lasting but for three days with only 110 exhibitors, was at *The Temple of Industry*, erected by Napoleon in 1798, in the Champs de Mars."[6] Napoleon was at the forefront of these early fairs (he was off capturing Egypt at the time) and kept them going once he became Emperor. That they came just ten years after the start of the French Revolution may reveal a hidden reasoning for these original fairs. The time after the Revolution had giant festivals such as the Festival of Law 1792 or the Festival of the Supreme Being in 1794, and there was a need to revise the history of France to suit its purposes.

*

1851 LONDON

London Crystal Palace 1851

The Great Exhibition of the Works of Industry of All Nations or thankfully shortened to *The Great Exhibition,* was held in Hyde Park, London, May 1 to October 15 1851. Joseph Paxton[7], a gardener and

---

[6]Bancroft. Napoleon is a big area in history to re examine, as so much of the standard story makes little sense, and generally seems made up.

[7] Oddly Paxton is credited with first cultivating the Cavendish banana, which has become basically the only banana eaten in the modern world. He later became rich, not from gardening or architecture, but from stock money made by railroad investments.

18

greenhouse builder won the contract to build the main building for the fair, and was assisted by railroad builders. Basically what they came up with was a massive glass and iron building that earned the nickname of The Crystal Palace. It was 1851 feet long (to correspond with the year of the fair) 450 feet wide, required 900,000 square feet of glass, and 3,300 iron columns. He modeled it on the leaf of the African water lily. It is claimed to have been completed in nine months, but of course there is no photographic record of this. What we do have is the drawings and photos of the building itself. It was enormous and contained over 13,000 exhibits for the fair, but there was far more. It had Egyptian temples, Babylonian temples, 1000's of Roman and Greek statues, concert halls, and giant trees to make you feel as if you were outdoors.

Interior London Crystal Palace

What I found very interesting was a speech given by Prince Albert in 1851 at a banquet given by the mayor of London, "*Nobody who has paid any attention to the particular features of our present era, will doubt for a moment that we are living at a period of most wonderful transition, which tends rapidly to accomplish that great end to which all history points, the realization of the unity of mankind, not a unity which breaks down the limits and levels the peculiar characteristics of the different nations of the earth, but rather a unity, the results and products of these very national varieties and antagonistic qualities.*" The two parts that strike me most of this excerpt is first the mention that progress comes from national and antagonistic qualities, hence warfare and conquest (exactly what the British and other European nations were doing at that time). The second is the mention of the time being a period of transition. I think this is a veiled statement to what was really going on at the time. A transition really was happening world wide between 1800 and 1900, and seems almost as if 1850 was some sort of marker. So much of any invention now a part of our world, somehow has its origins to some 'finding, inventing, understanding" after 1850. Its amazing once you begin to look for it. So the fact that the first fair took place in 1851 is indeed telling for me. As we will see in the last chapter on what is known as the added 1000 years, it could also be a similar idea in the 1800's.

Back to the Crystal Palace. An amazing six million people, around one/third of Britain's entire population at the time, visited the Exhibition. Its almost 200,000 pound profit was used to open the Victorian and Albert Museum, Science Museum, and Natural History Museum- each of course which are housed in gigantic Gothic looking palaces in an area that became known as Albertopolis.

The Crystal Palace was later moved in 1854 to Sydenham Hill in South London. The building was destroyed by fire on 30 November 1936. That will be a recurring theme, great building built in record time for exhibition, often burned in a fire afterwards. So successful was The Great Exhibition, that England had another one starting May 1, 1862. But no need to use the Crystal Palace again, no might as well build another giant new building at the Horticultural Society, this one which covered 23 acres, and consisted of two immense domes (each larger than St Peter's). Between the domes was a central avenue to see all the 28,600 exhibits and galleries.

*

NEW YORK-1853

New York Crystal Palace 1853

While not classified as a Worlds Fair, *The Exhibition of the Industry of All Nations* (known as the *New York Crystal Palace Exhibition*) basically was one. It was held at Bryant Park in 1853–54 in an iron-and-glass structure similar to the one in England. A 100 foot diameter dome topped it. It seems odd that the first two World Fairs, both had similar buildings named the Crystal Palace. Of course this building also burned down, on October 5, 1858. Unlike London, The Crystal Palace Fair of New York lost a lot of money. When it burned down a newspaper reported, "so bursts a bubble rather noteworthy in the annals of New York. To be accurate, the bubble burst some years ago, and this catastrophe merely annihilates the apparatus that generated it."[8]

Another Crystal Palace was built in Munich in 1854 for its Exposition. It was called the Glaspalast (Glass Palace). It lasted until 1931 when, you guessed it, a fire destroyed it. Then there was the Crystal Palace in Montreal, built for its 1860 Exhibition. It later included an ice rink inside during winter, housing one of the world's first hockey teams. It burnt down in 1880. Toronto had a Crystal Palace as well, a giant building built in 1878 for its annual Canadian Industrial Exhibition.

---

[8] Fair America by Robert Rydell, John Findling and Kimberly Pelle, Smithsonian Institute Press 2000 pg 17

It too would be destroyed by fire in 1906. Five Crystal Palace buildings, all destroyed in somewhat odd circumstances. I am sure there are more if one just digs into the world-wide Crystal Palace phenomena.

*

The people who put these fairs on really believed they were involved in some great upbringing of humanity, from primitive savages to good Victorian industrial Christians. Take this from Frank Morton Todd writing just after the San Francisco Fair of 1915, "*Expositions are not 'fairs,' and the merchandising element in them is merely a part of their financial support. They are what the name connotes: displays, demonstrations, vast exemplifications of the works of man; self conscious and intelligently directed. They are very modern. If those diligent merchants and manufacturers, the classic Greeks, had held them we should have had to exclaim, "What a marvelous people, to devise such an agency of progress...Read the chapter on 'A Single Handed Clock, and Boiling Eggs,' and you will understand how an exposition serves and speeds up human development. It is better to have the planned effects of one exposition than the accidental benefits of forty wars.*"[9] This message of the exposition actually a part of human progress, not a reflection of it, was common in these book overviews. They really believed that the fairs of the day were evolving the world. Fairs prior to World War One are called Industrial fairs, as they had a focus of technology, industry. Yet underlying all was the idea of the advancement of the Western World over "primitive" societies. For these early fairs the anthropology exhibits, basically natives shown off with their huts or tepees in a sort of zoo, were as much a feature of the fairs as the manufacturing exhibits or carnival attractions. The first fair to take this to the extreme, was the Philadelphia Exhibition of 1876.

*

PHILADELPHIA 1876

"*In different ways all of those fairs supported the proposition that the advance of the American industrial complex, as directed by an Anglo-Saxon elite, was synonymous with national progress.*"[10] Robert Rydell

[9]The Story of The Exposition, by Frank Morton Todd NY 1921
[10]Rydell p 25

Philadelphia, Main Building 1876

The first true World Fair in the US was the Philadelphia Exhibition of 1876 to celebrate the 100th anniversary of US Independence. At least that is how it liked to be known, but its official title at the time was *The International Exhibition of Arts, Manufactures, and Products of the Soil and Mine.* I am not fully sure how art and manufacture goes together with soil and mine (both of which would never make the title of any future exhibition) and Independence. Again the studylove site has links to several books of this fair, I recommend Centennial *Portfolio: a Souvenir of the International Exhibition* by Thompson Westcott (1876) which provides original drawings of all the buildings. Just for that it is a spectacular document.

Right after the US Civil War came the focus of big money capitalists who invested in the new industries of railroads, telegraph, and steel making. It was these new rich elite who were the ones to fund these fairs. "The wealthy supporters of world's fairs were interested not only in showing off their private wealth in a medium that they thought would help rebuild- literally reconstruct- the American Nation after the Civil War"...and to "propagate a particular view of the world that insisted on the presumed fact of Anglo-Saxon superiority as a way to unite whites, regardless of social class, at the expense of people defined racially as 'others'."[11]

---

[11]Rydell p19

Photo of a building actually under construction in 1875. Oddly this will become harder and harder to find as we go to future expositions.

A website named *free library of Philadelphia*[12] has over 800 drawings and photographs of this expo. And the construction photos are very telling in many cases, for unlike what we will see with the construction photos of other exhibitions- here are some of large inner wooden frames proving that some of the large buildings were temporary structures. However there are problems with many of the buildings such as Memorial Hall (the one building that made it through the fair) where the construction photo is more like what we will see in the future expos: that of a fully completed lower structure, some scaffolding, and work being done on an upper dome. It is the first photo of what becomes standard, photographs of completed lower levels surrounded by scaffolding.

The Philadelphia Exposition covered 285 acres, and was constructed in what becomes the very standard two years time frame. This fair occurred only ten years after the end of the Civil War, in a country supposedly recovering from all the damage, destruction and death of it. The main building was over 870,000 square feet (464 x 1880 feet), that is more than a third of a mile in length-similar to the Crystal Palace in London. It also included four 75-foot high towers with almost 700 columns. Unlike London which had only one main building, at

---

[12]libwww.freelibrary.org/digital/collection/home/page/10/id/centennial-exhibition

Philadelphia there was more. There was Machinery Hall with over 500,000 square feet of space, Agricultural Hall that looked like Cathedrals placed together (above each entrance was a beautiful set of rose windows). Of all the buildings in Philadelphia, only Memorial Hall (210 x 365 feet) still survives. It has a granite exterior and a 150 foot high dome. One top of the dome is a statue of Columbia (which we will see the importance of in the chapter on the Columbia Exhibition). The question we continue to ask is why build such large buildings, only to quickly tear them down when the expositions end?

Occidental.
Centennial.

The Transcontinental Hotel 1876, supposedly built for the Exposition, then torn down as soon as it was over.

But more was destroyed that just the Exposition itself. Research presented on stolenhistory[13] found that there were six giant hotels built next to the Exposition. They included the brick Grand Exposition Hotel (1,325 rooms), and the Globe Hotel which had 1,000 rooms. However this site[14] provides a very shocking revelation by stating, "All the hotels built for the exposition were demolished soon after its conclusion, except for the Unites States Hotel, which survived until the 1970's." This comment is exactly why I wrote this book. It is one thing to build some

---

[13]https://americasbesthistory.com/wfphiladelphia1876.html and presented to the forum by Shanda Hoffman
[14]https://philadelphiaencyclopedia.org/archive/hotels-and-motels/

fair buildings and tear them down, that is insane enough. But to also build a number of brick and stone hotels, and then tear them down as well is beyond insane. Would you not keep a few around and see if any of them still get guests, or does the city think that no one will ever want to visit Philadelphia again?

The Smithsonian took control of the new anthropological exhibits, and part of their job was to present the Native Indians as savage primitives compared to the civilized white Americans. These exhibits helped to provide a rationalization for the extreme violence taking place on the plains. This was the time of the final Indian wars, where entire villages being massacred, the buffalo slaughtered to near extinction, and germ warfare employed as diseases such as small pox were sent in on infected blankets. It would be this summer during the Fair that George Custer's 7th cavalry would suffer a complete defeat at the Little Big Horn which would create a call to "finish off the savages once and for all."

While there was a woman's building, Susan B Anthony felt this was no where near enough to help the unequal status of women (who could not vote), and on July 4 shocked the US Vice President at the fair by handing him a scroll containing "The Declaration of Rights of Women." African-Americans were offered no space at the fair, and in fact were not given any jobs (even those considered menial). This was to be a Fair for white people, by white people.[15]

Philadelphia 1876, Birds Eye Panorama[16]

I wish you could see the "birds eye diagram 1876" of Philadelphia in detail, the way it can be seen in online version, follow the footnote. Zoom in close. Not only can you see the colossal buildings of the Exposition on the left side, when you look at the main city of Philadelphia it is more like Florence. There is a mini coliseum, giant

[15]Rydell chapter 1
[16] Full panorama image can be found at https://upload.wikimedia.org/wikipedia/commons/0/0b/Panorama_of_Philadelphia_and_centennial_exhibition_grounds_LCCN2003679946.jpg

domes and spires, and in the center a building that looks exactly like the Parthenon. Again who was building this in less than 100 years that the city was in existence, and to this scale? Also look on the hill above the Exhibition grounds. You will see a tower structure with a ball on top. It looks exactly like a Tesla Tower. So were they using Tesla free-energy technology in 1876 to power this fair?

However the fair was a failure financially, as were most of the previous world's fairs, with the exception of London. The total cost for Philadelphia was $8,000,000, and the receipts were $4,300,000. Bancroft wrote in his book even with the money loss, "It is not, however, on the basis of dollars and cents that the success of such an effort can be estimated." He is claiming that the fairs are losing a lot of money- but that it is not a big deal. So why are they having them? We know what rich people like most is staying rich. They don't like dropping their money into things that lose money, and keep losing money. Thus the fairs can not be about money at all, but as Bancroft states "it is not on the basis of dollars and cents that success is estimated." The question then becomes what is? I believe it is to rewrite the complete historical narrative. To prop up the new white ruling elite (which I am not sure existed prior to 1800) and to destroy all of the old vestiges of the great civilizations that spanned the globe prior to the arrival of the "new conquerors." For that we have to look at some specific buildings supposedly built for some of the fairs.

*

STRANGE BUILDINGS

Hotel Internacional, Barcelona 1888

First is the Hotel Internacional or Gran Hotel Internacional that was supposed to have been built for the Universal Exposition of Barcelona in 1888. The hotel was 5,000 square meters, had capacity for 2,000 guests in 600 rooms and 30 apartments. According to the history sources, it was "built in a record time of 53 days." The construction began in the middle of December 1887, and the exterior was completed by February 14, 1888. To complete interior finishes is what required work until March. "In the middle of January, it was decided to work at night, using eighteen large electric lights, so the 650 masons, 100 carpenters and 40 plasterers could work around the clock."[17] Like all of these amazing Expo buildings, it was "a temporary facility to welcome visitors to the exhibition and was demolished once the fair was over." Supposedly modeled on the Ritz hotel in Switzerland, it was obviously meant to cater to high end guests.

---

[17] Wikipedia, Hotel Barcelona page

Hotel in 1888 to see the detail of ornamentation

Look at the scale of this building. It is giant. All of it covered with fine ornamentation. If you were going to build a temporary structure to tear down in a year, would you really go to all the trouble for the super fine finish on the exterior? No of course not. You simplify the build. You don't sculpt every square inch of the Duomo in Florence unless you expect the building to be there for many centuries. I asked a building contractor friend how long it would be build this today, with modern machines. He said it would be hard because of the ornamentation, but that likely it would take just over two years. Today with modern machines requires two years, but with horse, wagon, and hand screwdrivers was 53 days.

What makes the standard story even more unbelievable is that it is claimed to have no foundation, but placed on a metal structure to provide "stability" for the temporary building. Really no foundation! Do you really want 6,000 guests, particularly the rich elite of Europe, coming to stay and then die in your collapsed unsafe building? Come on, it's not even conceivable. And if the hotel is built that strongly...why the hell would you tear it down just one year later, on the date of May 1.[18]

---

[18] May 1, 1776 is claimed to be the date of the forming of the shadow group known as the Illuminati, who are claimed to be in control of every country and institution worldwide. Both of these dates, May 1 and 1776 have been given to other occasions (workers days, and the Independence of America) but both of these "celebratory" dates might actually be a reference to this Illuminati founding

My guess is that the work crew did not build anything, they were working on refurbishing a building that was already there. Perhaps they altered a few things, added a few things, and repainted it to look fresh. They did a major upgrade to it, which is conceivable to do in 53 days.[19]

*

BIRDS-EYE VIEW OF LOUISVILLE FROM THE RIVER FRONT AND SOUTHERN EXPOSITION, 1883.
DEDICATED BY THE PUBLISHERS TO THE LOUISVILLE BOARD OF TRADE AND MANUFACTURING INDUSTRIES.

Louisville Exhibition 1883

Next we look at the city of Louisville, which had a large regional exhibition beginning in 1883. Look at the size of the building in the center. It was a two-story wooden and glass structure designed by McDonald Brothers that covered approximately 12 acres, or three square blocks of the city. It was bigger than the Medici Palaces of Florence. The above drawing shows four interior courtyards with fountains that would have provided light and ventilation within the building. It also was decked out with "the largest installation of incandescent light bulbs, having been recently invented by Thomas Edison (a previous resident of Louisville). The fair had more incandescent lamps than all of New York City.[20]

---

[19] Ok that is one story, how about another? In Copenhagen Denmark they also had a fair in 1888. So of course they built a huge exhibition building next to Tivoli amusement park. Right after the fair it was torn down and the new City Hall built at the spot. Why would you build one thing, tear it down, then build another thing in a year?

When the yearly fairs ended in 1889, it was torn down and then used to build a small theater close by.[21] Why tear such a thing down? You could easily have some of the most beautiful apartments anywhere. The story lingering with the historians again is that the building was somehow temporary. But how temporary can a building be if you are going to use it five years in a row, and then use the very building materials to build another building? Or maybe it wasn't temporary.

The city of Louisville is supposed to be founded in 1778 during the American Revolution. Yes in the middle of the great War of Independence, founding a new city was considered a good idea. That sounds odd. Eighty civilians and 150 soldiers were said to have gone there to start it. Are we really to believe that in 100 years they went from log cabins to that. Now perhaps they did, but it really needs to be examined further as to how the material was quarried, transported and raised in a place with no roads, trucks or machines. Recall the word founded is actually the two combined words "found" and "dead." And most US cities were "founded" in the period 1700 to 1850. More bizarre are cities like Salt Lake City (supposedly founded by Mormon pioneers in 1850) or San Francisco (by gold rush cowboys in 1847). Yet in 20 years they have a city with cathedrals, palaces, towers, and domes that would rival Cologne or Prague? Cowboys and soldiers in 20 years recreated old Europe. The story is the same for most every North American city, be it Toronto or Indianapolis.

---

[20] Went to the Exhibition tonight, by Kathryn Ann Bratcher, Filson Historical Society website

[21] The theater lasted until 1916 when it too was torn down.

From St Louis Fair Book showing Evolution of the Races

At the New Orleans Cotton Fair of 1884, the Smithsonian set up a presentation that all races were symbolic of a human life span, and the blacks and natives were at the children stage, while the whites were in the adult stages. They also set up comparisons of native skulls and the skulls of criminals (which were presented as small thus similar) compared to the large skulls of white people. Early fairs, when the did present exhibits on American blacks, it was to show how good of agriculture and industrial workers they were, not that there should be any social equality for them. I have included the front piece of the book by Buel on Anthropology because of what the description of the image presents, "*The photogravure herewith is from an excellent specially prepared drawing which very accurately illustrates, as nearly as the science of ethnology is able to, the characteristic types of mankind arranged in a progressive order of development from primitive or prehistoric man to the highest example of modern civilization. the two central figures are symbolical, representing intelligence with the torch of Enlightenment and the book of Wisdom, invading the darksome cave in which ignorance skulks in companionship with bird of evil omen and superstition. it is aspiration lighting the dungeon of savagery and directing the race to better conditions, moral, intellectual and social.*"[22] This pretty much sums up the attitude of the Western nations to the rest of the world at that time, much of which continues to this day.[23]

*

Sydney Exhibition Hall 1879

So how about Australia. That is another country with a recent European founding. It has the same story, within less than 50 years a group of soldiers and convicts have created a massive building program. Above is the Garden Palace for the 1879 Sydney International Exhibition. It was designed by James Barnett and constructed by John Young (who helped build the London Crystal Palace, what luck!). The dome was 100 feet in diameter and 210 feet high. The building had a floor space of over 112,000 meters. The Palace cost of £191,800 and was completed in eight months, the reason given for the quick build was due to import of electric lighting from England which allowed work to happen 24 hours a day. Instead of this looking like the Crystal Palace it was created to be like that of a large cathedral with included towers and giant central dome. Surprise surprise, it was destroyed in a fire on September 22, 1882.

Melbourne had their International Exhibition a year later, and used many of the same exhibits as Sydney. Their Royal Exhibition

---

[22]Buel, Louisiana and the Fair volume 4
[23]Rydell p29

Building was built in the Victorian Gardens, and for some odd reason this building WAS NOT temporary. It was kept and used again for an Exhibition in 1888, and parts of it still remain today in a World Heritage Exhibition building. One again has to wonder how recently arrived convicts, with little building skill or tools, are able to construct incredible things in record times. Look up the list of what was built in Christchurch New Zealand 1851-53 for example, where 300 inhabitants, mostly women and children, build massive structures like cathedrals.

*

Before moving on I must make mention of the International Exhibition of Paris in 1889. "So vast was the scale and yet so artistic the design that it became the wonder of the civilized nations of earth, and by all it was conceded that never before had been witnessed such a combination of the grand and beautiful in science, art, and industry." Interspersed among the main structures were groups representing foreign lands; a street in Algiers, a Turkish village, the minarets of Tunis, and the dwellings of New Caledonia.

"While the art galleries formed one of the most interesting features of this effort, it surpassed, as I have said, all its predecessors as a great international exposition, with a larger scope and variety of exhibits than had ever before portrayed the phases of human industry. There were probably but few who could examine and fewer still who could appreciate in their entirety the treasures and attractions of this great spectacular display. To make the circuit merely of the grounds and buildings, the former occupying 173 and the latter 75 acres, required a journey of fifteen miles, and to form an intelligent estimate of their contents needed months of close observation and study."[24] Recall this fair happened just 18 years after much of Paris was supposedly destroyed in 1871 by the Germans during the Franco-Prussian war.

The great building of this fair was the Eiffel tower, 894 feet in height, still one of the attractions of Paris. However, it does not now look like it did when it was first built. Notice in the construction photo above that can be seen some rounded structures along the first level. These could be seen in photos during the 1900 Exposition as well. Then a decade later they vanish. So what are these? They were part of the original design, so why remove them? I think they may have been part of making the Tower its full original purpose, as part of an energy-

---

[24]Bancroft

generating device, a device that for some reason after the World Fairs was shut off. I will discuss the towers for energy in the upcoming chapters.

*

But we must look ahead to the Great Expositions after Paris, and in fact the cities that held them, for we come across massive buildings are claimed to have gone up faster than what we can do with modern machines. To recall where this investigation is headed, a) the buildings were already there from long before and just needed to be refurbished and or restored, or b) there was a technology at the time that is not reported or believed, one we may just rediscovering today.

CHAPTER 3
PLANNING AND BUILDING
Chicago

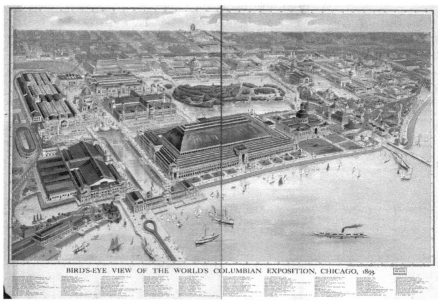

BIRD'S-EYE VIEW OF THE WORLD'S COLUMBIAN EXPOSITION, CHICAGO, 1893.

Birds Eye View of Columbian Exposition, 1893

Starting in 1893 there were nine major exhibitions in the US: Chicago 1893, Nashville 1897, Omaha 1898, Buffalo 1901, St Louis 1904, Portland 1905, Jamestown 1907, Seattle 1909, and San Francisco in 1915. I will examine the background of the Expositions and the supposed magic construction of them. The cities themselves have magic building stories as well, and this too must be examined as the history of the Expos and the cities they were held in are linked.

Chicago's Exhibition of 1893 (shown above) was a 690 acre site, built supposedly from scratch in two years- which included all the planning, landscaping, construction of the buildings, all the canals dug, all the roads and sidewalks put in, and all the midway rides up and running. What sort of planning does that require? Even if you claim to have 100,000 workers to do the job (Chicago claimed to use 40,000). Who was setting up the feeding of them every day? Where did all the bathrooms go? How did the materials get to the site, with no machines, trucks, or electrical power? That is 690 acres of not just buildings, but monster buildings. Look at the Manufactures Building in the center, by itself it is 30 acres. How can you build this stuff so fast?

I presented this question to my building contractor friend, can the entire Columbian Exposition of 1893 be built in two years today? After surveying the photos his first response was a simple "No, not possible."

"Not possible," I asked back.

Then he looked more closely at the hundred or so photos I showed to him, "Look, it would take two years just to have the architectural and landscaping plans drawn up. This is a complex building project, and it has to be planned out properly, you cant just start throwing things up without having a good plan of where everything is going to be and why. How are those lakes are going to be made, dug out and set up to be sure there is no flooding...Then you need two years to do the landscaping and make the lakes and canals and roads...and I mean two years with modern equipment. Then you can get to the buildings. At least more ten years for that."

"So 10-15 years with modern machines," I asked.

"Give or take, yeah. If I had the 50,000 guys, all the machines I wanted, and an unlimited budget of hundreds of millions of dollars, then ya maybe 10 years. Maybe longer."

"Do you have any idea how this could have been done in two years between 1891 to 1893?"

"Again like I said, with the technology available at the time, it's just not possible. So for this to be true, this project equals the building of the pyramids in Egypt."

But that is not the story presented by historians for the Chicago Exposition, which the planning meetings are said to have been done in one month- and the entire exposition finished in less than two- including losing time for severe winters. The story makes no sense. So what is that story you ask...well this chapter is devoted to sharing not just the story of building this Exposition, but the city of Chicago as well.

*

CHICAGO'S HISTORY

Chicago Federal Building, 1911

Yes the building you are looking at is in Chicago, or it was in Chicago. This was the Federal Building, claimed to have been built between 1898 and 1905...just after the Exposition ended. Talk of Grandeur and amazement, this was it. And right away one would need to ask, just how was it built at the time? Because this was not a "temporary structure" this was full of marble and stone columns and a giant dome. How many thousands of horses would be needed to move the shovels of dirt, how many tens of thousands of men digging and hauling stone? How do you build that in 1898. And of course why? Why is something like that needed? And needed in every city in the United States of that period. Of course it survived only until 1966, when it was torn down to build that building below, The Kluczynski Federal Building. Why!

New Chicago Federal Building, 1970

Of course it would be easy to make this a simple case of comparing "old world architecture" to modern architecture. That does come into play. I want to be clear that buildings like the Old Chicago Federal Building were in fact ancient art in stone. It holds the same principles of geometry, harmonic proportion, and energy creation that can be found at the Parthenon, Luxor Temple or Chartres. Modern buildings are not. While I will present the difference between ancient and modern art at the end of this book, this chapter is a historical look at the origins of these cities. How fast they were built up, almost "magically," looking like postcards of Ancient Rome. Then the buildings either get burnt down in fires that do not at all seem like fires, or get demolished to build things like the Kluczynski Building. A few of these old marvels continue on today labeled "museum," "university," or "court house." What survives is just a small portion of what was.

*

The historical story of Chicago claims that French explorers first came to the area in the late 1600's, finding only local Algonquin Natives. A fort was built and a few log homes, but none of the wooden structures were said to make it through the War of 1812.[25] It was only when the

---

[25] The wars of 1812, which was basically the first modern world war, and are an important marker event and will be the subject of a future book.

city was "incorporated" by big northern businessmen in 1837, due to the fact the spot would be a central point on an east-west transport system, that the city really began. This historical presentation means that EVERY building that has ever been in Chicago must only have been built after 1837. By the time of the 1893 Worlds Fair, Chicago was a city of massive hotels, towers, domes, and Roman columns. All built supposedly in less than sixty years. Which would be amazing achievement if it were not that most the city was burned down in the Great Fire of 1871. But I will get into the fires shortly, for now we are looking at the origin in Chicago and its Roman-like buildings.

The name of Chicago itself is the first problem I have with this city's history. The standard historical claim is that it was a French rendering of the Native American word shikaakwa, a type of onion. The place name "Checagou" was found in a memoir by Robert de LaSalle in 1679, while Henri Joutel's journal of 1688 noted that the wild garlic, called "chicagoua", grew abundantly in the area. Supposedly this was a native village because this place provided a fairly short portage between Lake Michigan and the Mississippi River system. So that is the story, native settlement with a name derived from a type of onion and no building until whites take total control in 1837. However early maps tell a different story.

One of the greatest tools for the revisionist historian is ancient maps, because they show a level of detail and perfection in most cases that they are not supposed to have (for they were often based on much older maps from perhaps as far back as the Ancient Egypt, kept in secure ares such as the Vatican). There are discrepancies on the maps, generally presented as mistakes by the early map makers, "they just were not wise enough to know the world they were mapping," the standard historical answer. But they got most of the map perfect, leading to question about areas the are today in question.

Other maps such as the first world map of 1587 by Urbano Monte depict what can only be called cities (with Italian names) all across North America. I don't think he would have just popped down a bunch of native Indian villages onto such a map (for they have a similar marking and symbols to those in continental Europe). It is more likely that when he was making that map, information on what was in North America was well known, and as such, placed on this very accurate early map. And the name of a large settlement known as Chicagou is right where you would expect Chicago to be today. Some maps such as the 1596 Debry Map show the name Chilaga where Chicago should be. Even today Chilaga is thought of by historians as a mythical place like Camelot.[26] Like the mythological Troy becoming a real place, perhaps Chilaga is real too.

Chicago depicted in 1832, nothing but log homes

This drawing is supposed to show the time before any major building had begun, in 1832 when there was a population of 2,000. Interestingly you can see that the drawing was made in 1892...right at the time that the buildings of the World's Fair were "being completed." How convenient! This is a good example of how history might possibly be just made up, that the World Fair wanted an historical story, and so such drawings were created to help provide it.

---

[26] This map also includes the name Chiogigua, west of an island city in the middle of a lake Conibaz, which is NW of Chilaga. Could that Lake have been modern Winnipeg labeling that city as the ancient Chiogigua? Interestingly Debry created many illustrations of the early North America, Indian villages, and the Spanish "invasion." In several illustrations I have found that what can only be called dinosaurs are along the Indian shorelines. So far no explanation for this depictions have been provided.

Chicago 1853

And this is supposed to be Chicago in 1853. That is a massive amount of building for less than 20 years. I am counting five major towers similar to cathedrals, several other smaller ones, and round tower buildings. How was all this built in just twenty years, from a population of 2,000? Where did the building materials come from? How did the materials get in with only dirt roads to move what would be massive amounts of stone and brick? I can say stone and brick as photos coming up from 1858 show downtown and almost no wood at all. The fire story gets harder to explain. Brick and stone is a much longer building process, and this size just can not be built up in twenty years. But that is not the real strange part. How about the story that they lifted, yes lifted up, all of the buildings from street level during the next ten years.

Drawing of the raising of Chicago Briggs House (1 oF 2)

The history basically states that Chicago was built on a swamp, and had poor drainage (for it had no high ground compared to the lake edge). The poor drainage led to standing water which led to epidemics of typhoid, dysentery and cholera. A quote from Paul Johnson in *the History of the American People* "The city was built in a low-lying area subject to flooding. In 1856 the city council decided that the entire city should be elevated four to five feet by using a newly available jacking-up process. In one instance, the 5-story Briggs Hotel, weighing 22,000 tons, was lifted while it continued to operate." Johnson reminded that such a feat could not have happened in Europe and wrote "this astounding feat was a dramatic example of American determination and ingenuity: based on the conviction that anything material is possible."[27]

This is the presentation of it at Wikipedia, *"In January 1858, the first masonry building in Chicago to be thus raised—a four-story, 70-foot (21 m) long, 750-ton (680 metric tons) brick structure situated at the north-east corner of Randolph Street and Dearborn Street—was lifted on two hundred jackscrews to its new grade, which was 6 feet 2 inches (1.88 m) higher than the old one, 'without the slightest injury to the building.'... Before the year was out, they were lifting brick buildings more than 100 feet (30 m) long."* Yet this is just a warm up. In 1860 they raised up half a city block on Lake Street, between Clark Street and LaSalle Street; a solid masonry row of shops, offices, printeries, etc., 320 feet (98 m) long, comprising brick and stone buildings, some four stories high, some five, having a footprint taking up almost one acre (4,000 m2) of space, and an estimated all in weight including hanging

[27]Wikipedia raising Chicago page

sidewalks of thirty-five thousand tons. Businesses operating out of these premises were not closed down for the lifting; as the buildings were being raised, people came, went, shopped and worked in them as if nothing out of the ordinary was happening. In five days the entire assembly was elevated 4 feet 8 inches (1.42 m) in the air by a team consisting of six hundred men using six thousand jackscrews, ready for new foundation walls to be built underneath. The spectacle drew crowds of thousands, who were on the final day permitted to walk at the old ground level, among the jacks."[28] Basically the claim is that the whole of downtown, the streets, sidewalks and buildings were raised on hydraulic jacks or jackscrews. While the people were still living and working in the buildings. Think of that. Not even send them away for a few days, oh no, let them just walk in and up the 5 flights of stairs while the building is being lifted up. That is how ludicrous the story is.

Bancroft describes the raising as, "*this work was in truth a necessity, in order to provide a thorough system of sewerage, and to avoid the malarial fevers and other forms of sickness caused by the low, swampy site, a site which for years after Chicago had become a thriving commercial town was little better than a quagmire, and where, as one of her citizens remarked, 'the one unequaled, universal, inevitable, invincible thing about the place was – mud.'* (my reference) *To accomplish this task the streets were filled in, and by means of jack-screws worked by steam power, not only the largest dwellings, but the largest business buildings and business blocks, together with churches, theatres, hotels, and edifices of every kind, were raised to the required elevation, and that without begin vacated, whether used for business or residence purposes.*" Then the workers diverted the entire river system "by an extraordinary feat of engineering was made to change its course, its southern branch being connected, at a distance of two and a half miles from the lake front, with the Illinois and Michigan canal, which has also been so much deepened as to draw the waters of the lake."[29]

OK, either this is a work that rivals building the Giza pyramids, or this is just a giant fairy tale. I don't see an in between with this. First to build an entire city on a swamp? With giant buildings that would require massive foundations only to realize, oh gee were are on a swamp, better raise them all up then. So raise all the buildings, and in fact the streets as well- divert the river, and build new canals. Does anyone

---

[28]Wikipedia raising Chicago
[29]Bancroft

really believe this? Think of trying to do that today, it would be a major undertaking that might not be possible even with all of our modern machinery. Yet Chicago could do this in 1858? Again go ask your local building contractor to raise up say a small city, like South Bend Indiana-population 100,000. See what they tell you from, "what?" to "oh you have fifty years and two billion dollars."

Besides I have only found two photographs of this being done, mostly there are only poorly-made drawings. They had photography at this time, there are a lot of photographs from the 1850's available. Floods in California and Civil War dead[30] are photographed. Many very average things were photographed. Would not something like this, something that had never even been attempted in human history not warrant interest for a couple of photographs?

Actual photo of the supposed raising of the Briggs House. (2 ᴼᖴ 2)

The above is one of those actual photographs. As you can see it is basically the same view as the drawing presented on the previous page. The drawing may in fact come directly from this photo. Yet they are totally dissimilar. The drawing has it made out like hundreds of jacks are lifting the building off a very flat and level street ground. But here I see nothing being raised and no jacks, instead what seems like the building has been dug out and they are trying to lay a foundation of

---

[30]Though many consider the shots of the war including those of dead soldiers to be staged. Not on image of anything resembling a battle has been found.

some type beneath it. What can only be described as a pile of dirt is next to it, but that could have also been a sink hole (now filled in) that they tried to keep the building from falling into.

One more strange mention on this topic. There is suggestion that a specific engineer John C Lane was a key element in making this work,. He was supposed to have learned his building lifting techniques in San Francisco in 1853. What? As we will see further on, San Francisco should have just been founded in 1847. There should be a few gold miners and cowboys there, and a few simple shacks to accommodate them. What buildings are there that would need to be raised? There should be no buildings at all there. But some standard historical sources do claim there were buildings long before 1847, and quite spectacular.

View north from court dome, part of Hesler Panorama 1858, University of Illinois

The above view is one of eight photograph parts that make up a panorama of Chicago taken from the dome of the Court house in 1858. The entire panorama can be seen at the chicagology website. Wooden buildings is the claim for why the city burnt so easy in the 1871 fire. Yet I see almost all brick and stone (just what we will find in the aftermath of the fire photos). Secondly note that this entire area (along with the eight other photos) is supposed to have been raised 10 feet during this

46

period. I hope this is beginning to be seen just how crazy this idea even is.

A few paragraphs ago I made emphasis on one word of Bancroft's book, mud. This is but a throw away line in Bancroft's writing, but it may be a direct reflection that the city was covered in mud. There is a group of current researchers of something called the "mudflood." They link to a world wide burying of cities in mud during this period (17 to 1800's). Mudflood will be defined fully in the final chapter, but to me it is more likely in the 1850's that Chicago was not using a workforce to raise the buildings from a swamp, but rather to dig it out of what may have been a river of mud that buried much of it. No matter, the story of raising all the buildings of Chicago is covering up something (no pun intended), and that is again why this examination of Worlds Fairs is so important. Something is very wrong with our history of this period of time, and every part of it that we can uncover, might finally take us that next key step to knowing what really happened to the world.

*
FIRES

Two after views of the 1871 Chicago Fires

      On October 8,1871 Chicago has what is known as its Great Fire. Bancroft described it as, "it had destroyed more than 17,000 buildings, and more than 70 miles of pavement; it had blotted out of existence the entire business section, most of the railroad depots with their rolling-stock, most of the docks and much of the shipping, while of all the public edifices of which Chicago was wont to be proud, her courthouse and post office, her custom-house and chamber of commerce, their remained only here and there the lurid skeleton of a wall. There were not a dozen wholesale stores left standing in the city; there were few hotels, theaters, or churches, and there was but a single bank."

There are many questions. First is that there were four other great fires that same day all around Lake Michigan (one killing 2,500 people) suggesting a common source (some suggest a meteor strike in the region). More deeply, when you see photos after any of the fires (such as Chicago above), it looks more like it has been bombed rather than a fire. What we see in the images are remains of brick and stone, basically blown out- not showing fire damage of wood. Think of the heat that would be required to actually burn brick or stone, meanwhile wooden utility poles are everywhere and have not been touched. In other cities trees are fine right beside buildings totally blown apart. Originally I was going to have a short discussion of the oddity of this fire- but the fact that EVERY city in North America has a great fire during this period- and that the photographs all produce questions and not many answers, I felt the discussion had to be moved to be included in the final chapter of this book. For now keep in mind that whatever this disaster was, most of the city- and its buildings are supposed to have been destroyed.[31]

I will leave you with a couple more images for your inspection. The first is the weirdest building I have ever come across.

---

[31] Interestingly just 10 days after the Chicago fire of 1871, a map of the city was published in Harper's Weekly Magazine (October 21 edition) supposedly drawn by Theodore Davis. What is odd is that none of the magnificent type buildings (columns, domes, towers that can be seen in the map of 1853) are present in this map. This highly likely indicates the map could be fraudulent and its publication part of presenting a false historical narrative to the population.

This is a photo of the old Chicago City Hall, which was torn down in 1908. This was supposed to have been built in 1853 along Randolph and Lasalle Streets when the need for a City Hall became more than the needs of their small original one. Interesting fact Abraham Lincoln's body was placed here during his funeral in 1865. I don't think that is by accident. It is in fact a message. But what is this? You have what looks like the first floor, on the second floor- and a completely different building, made of completely different material on the bottom. I have seen a lot of this in Ancient Egypt like Luxor, where one temple is built upon the ruins of another and so on. Is that what we are looking at here. Two successive civilizations having built on top. It is just baffling to say the least. Again my building contractor was very clear- "this is two distinct buildings," he said. "See this bottom one is not the same as the top. I would say this bottom one is at least 50 years older than the top, maybe 100." When I told him the history that they were built as one in the 1850's he responded, "I don't care about history, these are two different buildings from two different time periods. Very strange."

New Chicago City Hall in 1914 postcard

But then they just tore the thing down and built a new city hall, the one that still stands today, and is pictured above in an early postcard. Interestingly it has a fasces sign over top of the main entrance. General history calls it a bundle of wood with an axe on top, that was used as a symbol of the highest most powerful ruler. Mussolini and Hitler adopted this symbol as a key element of their political movements, and the word fascism comes from it. However recent research is changing the view of a fasces from a symbol, to a possible powerful energy weapon (where Tesla got his death ray from). Instead of wood we may have some sort of metal rods, surrounded not by rope but by copper wire. The trumpets that took down the walls of Jericho were not simple trumpets, but energy weapons of which the fasces might be be symbolizing. Thus much of the world's great architecture could be a counter-measure to such energy weapons. Not only could cathedrals generate free energy for cities, they could also be used to block energy weapons. Do not forget the story of when Cathar cites such as Beziers were attacked by the invading Christian crusaders, they all went to the cathedral for shelter. They may be more of a reason for this than first believed. And the fasces is found all over the USA. Look at the Lincoln Memorial in Washington, the two sides of the chair he sits in are a pair of fasces.

But again this gets odd when you take a look at where the modern city hall is located. Right across the street is the very strange Chicago Temple Building, the site of The First United Methodist Church.

51

This, the tallest church in the world, was built between 1922-24. Clarence Darrow of Monkey-trial fame had an office on the sixth floor. One block the other way is an almost a step pyramid like structure with a dome on top of it. Two streets over is one with a glass pyramid on top. A few blocks to the river is a giant domed building on North Wabash that has secondary high domes at each corner.

There is far more to explore with the odd history of what was built in Chicago after 1893, but right now I want to get to the planning and constructing of the Exposition itself, before returning to look at what else was "supposed" to be built in Chicago at the very same time.

*
EXHIBITION CONSTRUCTION 1891-1893

Machinery Hall, 1893. How and when were buildings like this constructed?

In 1890 US politicians wanted to hold a fair to better the one that had just completed in Paris the previous year. The new fair was to show the world the rise of America and that it had become, according to John Findling, "The apex of world's civilization." Ie the new Roman Empire. They chose to honor and celebrate Christopher Columbus. The myth of the Spanish guy sailing in 1492 to "discover" the new world was a key part of the Exposition presentation, and of historical teaching at this time. But can one claim to discover a land that has perhaps 40 million native people already living there? Within three hundred years almost all of those native in North and South America were killed or turned into slaves by Spaniards, French and British/Americans. What Christopher Columbus represents is not discovery, but what was in fact an armed assault on a continent by Europe. The question is which myth of Columbus were the Exposition organizers really attempting to present; the outward tale of European discovery, or European colonialism and slaughter?

Many US cities lobbied to hold the fair, but it came down to the two largest: Chicago and New York. There was supposed to be a rather nasty back room fight about it, between big Chicago business men such as Charles H. Schwab, Chicago railroad barron John Whitfield Bunn (who had Abraham Lincoln as his attorney prior to the Civil War), and Chicago banker Lyman Gage who battled New York's big money magnets, J. P. Morgan, Cornelius Vanderbilt, and William Waldorf Astor. The Chicago group won out. One of the main selling points for the Chicago group was presenting the way the city had risen from the ashes of the Great Fire of 1871, thus also embarking symbolism of the Egyptian Phoenix. This symbol also represented the United States, they they were the new great civilization, rising from the ashes of the previous "primitive societies" that they had just conquered. These fairs was going to be the elite's way to let the world know it. Or at least, make the average American believe it.

Burnham and Root, in a photo dated 1890, less than one year before John Root would be dead.

53

The first problem was where to hold the Exposition in Chicago. Many wanted it to be on the prairie outskirts with lots of land, while other protested that the prairie landscape too dull for a fair. Frederick Law Olmsted, the man who set the design for New York's Central Park and the landscaping of the George Washington Masonic National Memorial Grounds, was the one brought in to finalize a site. He chose Jackson Park. At the time the area was considered a swamp on the Lakeshore. The Architect firm of Burnham and Root was given the contract to design the fair itself. However just one year after getting the contract, John Root died, leaving Daniel Burnham to be the sole architect for the firm (whose name of Root was quickly removed) and also for the fair. It is odd was that Root died just five days after the first main architect meeting in January 1891. Was it just co-incidence, or was Root somehow against the main plan and had to be "eliminated"? Even more odd was that partner of Olmsted, Henry Sargent Codman, would die two years later on January 13, 1893 at the age of 28 as the result of an operation for an attack of appendicitis.

Burnham is an odd character. He grows up in the New Church of Swedenborg. His family moves to Chicago in the 1850's. He tries to get into Yale and Harvard but is denied, and instead learns drafting at an architecture firm. He tries being a gold miner, druggist, and glass salesman. Then he meets Root on the street and they decide to start their own architecture firm, with basically no experience. He knew only drafting, Root had studied in England and New York, but he also was only working as a draftsman. They had designed nothing, nor studied architecture. Within weeks of this chance meeting (which I believe is nothing but a fairy tale) they get a contract from the richest man in Chicago, head of the Union Stockyards, John B Sherman, to build his mansion. Supposedly while doing the work Burnham meets Sherman's daughter and marries her. So this nobody who failed at everything, and has no experience and no money, just magically marries the richest man's daughter, and designs his mansion. It was through Sherman that he began to get contracts. He is credited with being the architect of 14.7 million square feet of buildings in New York, Chicago, Washington, San Francisco, Cincinnati, Detroit, Manila among others. Just how does anyone actually have the time to do that? He was also the architect for the the Montauk and Masonic Temple buildings in Chicago. So that is lots of Masonic architects in charge of the fair planning. Don't forget that Montauk was the name of the base used by the US Navy in supposed time travel experiments in Long Island in the 1970's. In 1908 Burnham published a book that laid out the plan for the city of Chicago's future. Oddly he also made up a series of plans for San Francisco in 1905. His plans, which were to be followed, were supposedly scrapped due to the 1906 earthquake.

George R Davis was the director general and got help with the exhibits from R Brown Goode of the Smithsonian, which was founded in 1847 at its castle headquarters. Why there is a castle in that location in 1847 no one is explaining well, or just how the castle was built. Today the Smithsonian is the North American equivalent of the Vatican. The Vatican hides almost 50 miles long worth of book and manuscripts that no one is allowed to see, the Smithsonian hides historical treasures of the original narrative of the Americas. Actually the entire story of the founding of the Smithsonian is bizarre to say the least, but I leave that for you to study on your own.

Burnham's friend Frank Millet was chosen as the decorations director for the Exposition. It is he who is credited with inventing the spray painting technique to "whitewash" the buildings to paint them white in record time. Of course I have some questions about this as well. The word "whitewash" has the meaning of deception, double cross and deceit. It was first used in Medieval England to discuss painting old buildings white to hide their age and erosion. So was he paining temporary buildings to look uniform, or painting some temporary buildings along with original structures who were already eroded so that people would be unable to tell the difference. Oddly Burnham and Millet were tied in death. In 1912 Burnham was sailing on the SS Olympic from New York to Heidelberg at the exact same time that Millet was on the Titanic sailing to the US. Yes that Titanic. Millet died on the Titanic, Burnham died in Heidelberg 47 days later, supposedly of food poisoning.

Burnham is quoted as saying he wanted to build the Columbia Exhibition as an example of a "prototype of what he thought a city should be." It was to be designed to follow Beaux Arts principles, namely French neoclassical architecture principles based on symmetry, balance, and splendor. What that basically means is that it should look like Ancient Rome. The buildings at this fair are credited with the building style of the US for the next twenty years. My belief is that the Beau Arts architecture movement was created in order to produce specific architects who could build old-style buildings to be placed beside the much older originals so that no one could tell the difference between ancient and modern. Recall Kundera's quote from the last chapter, how it can take just but a generation for people to totally lose their knowledge of the past.

Here is a telling quote from Bancroft, "*Before even the foundations could be laid of any of the Exposition buildings proper, a vast amount of expensive preliminary work was necessary, on account of the nature of the site and its distance from sources of supply. The marsh lands must be drained by the construction of artificial water-ways connecting with the lake, and utilized in adding to the landscape effect of the grounds adjacent...For grading and filling purposes, 1,200,000 cubic yards of earth must be handled at a cost of nearly $500,000...railroad track and rolling stock for the transportation of materials required; viaducts, bridges, and piers, improvements on the lake front, water supply, sewerage, and gas pipes. Then there were buildings for construction purposes, with stores and boarding-houses for the accommodation of thousands of workmen; there were fire and police stations;... all to be provided for before the real work on construction was begun.*" Just read that carefully. That is what had to occur before any building construction could actually start. A few landscapers I spoke with suggested that even with modern machinery, it would take around two or three years just to lay over the swamp to prepare for buildings, along with digging out the lagoons and canals. My contractor gave two years for planning and perhaps 5 to 7 years for the buildings. So did they have some magic wizard to make all this happen in two years?

Added to that was weather problems. The winters of 1891 and 92 were full of extreme cold and heavy snowfalls, which supposedly even caved in some of the new roofs of buildings. "Even under this disadvantage work was continued as usual, and with such energy that by the close of January, 1893, not only the principal structures, but many of the state and foreign buildings were practically completed." Thus not only is one dealing with no roads or trucks for bringing in materials, an entire swamp that basically needed all the work done listed in the paragraph above, but was also felled by long stretches of extreme winter where work was stalled. Yet two years is all that was needed.

Laying foundation on the Jackson Park swamp.

However one thing is certain, the place chosen for the fair is indeed a bit of a swamp. To support the many structures tens of thousands of wooden pillars were driven into the mud to be the foundation for the fair. Now we do have photos of this going on, so we know this was done for at least some buildings. But for all of them? Like the massive Manufacturers Building was held up by a few thousand logs on top of a swamp? What of the Liberal Arts Building (the only building supposedly built to last) and still standing today. Is it standing on a foundation of wood pilings? I would assume not, thus I would really like to examine the foundation of that building for that would give more of a clue at to how the rest of them were constructed.

Women's Building, 1893

What was odd is that Bancroft presents that all preliminaries for the foundations of Jackson Park were not completed until the summer of 1891, and then quite casually remarks, "and the foundation laid of the Woman's Building, the first to be taken in hand"...and later, "The Woman's Building was the only one under roof; the brick walls of the Art palace were still unfinished, and the Manufactures Building had not risen above its thirty and a half acres of floor." Does that mean what I think it means? He is claiming that Woman's Building was built before all the others? Bancroft also wrote, "Said the Chicago correspondent of a leading San Francisco journal, writing from Jackson Park in February, 1893: 'This seems to be an impossibility. To be sure, those in charge claim that they will be ready on time. Still the cold-blooded fact stares one in the face that only the Woman's Building is anywhere near completion inside and out.'" It seems almost certain based on this information that the Woman's Building was already there at the site. At a time when not one other structure had been started. So what else was at the site before construction began?

But Bancroft does not stop there, as he continues his poetic references about the construction, "*While the buildings were in process of construction one could almost realize the colossal proportions of this enterprise. Entering the grounds in the spring of 1892, the visitor beheld such a scene of bustling activity as that which at the founding of Carthage greeted the father of the Roman race when first he set foot on Punic shores. And yet it was a silent activity that pervaded this groups of mammoth structures, while pillars and walls and domes were rising around him. Here was an army of mechanics, with hammer and saw and mallet, all plying their tools with the vigor of a true American workman; but amid the wide spaces that separated these huge architectural efforts the noise was barely perceptible. Then there was an air of unreality about this congregation of edifices, so strange in dimensions and design, rising as from the touch of a fairy's wand at the bidding of some potent agency.*"

Again we have some very odd choice of wording. While comparing it to the founding of Carthage is odd, what struck me most was that twice in this rambling he mentioned that the workmen were making no noise. Why were the workmen making no noise? Building is very very noisy, even without modern machines. On the surface his quote seems to suggest that the buildings were so far away from each other as to not hear one being constructed from the other. However if we read between the lines, this can also be a sly reference that there were lots of workmen, but rather than building they were restoring. Restoring work (as I have had the chance to witness in Egypt) is very quiet. Lastly he states that the buildings "have risen from a fairy's wand." Thus arisen magically. Which could be a way of again presenting slyly that the buildings were already there, for without any noise or work and set by magic, there just appeared. That is exactly the same "poetic" style the Inca or Maya described to the Spanish how such structures like Macchu Picchu or Teotihuacan were built by the race of people long before the Inca or Maya came to them.

The website Friendsofthewhitecity presented this, which I am guessing comes from a Chicago Tribune article after the fair was over, "*Work on the Jackson Park site began on the morning of February 11, 1891 by Dennis Madden and a group of 30 Italian workers. Madden was a foreman for McArthur Bros. which was the contractor awarded the project of dredging, draining and grading the Jackson Park site. The Italian workers were supplied by a local agency...The first worker, who because of his anonymity could represent the immigrant forefather of all immigrant Italian families who called Chicago home at the end of the 19th century, raised his pick and swung it three times before making a small hole in the frozen earth. The other 29 Italians followed suit and the transformation of Jackson Park had begun...The work of building the Expo was heavily dependent on manual labor and at the height of construction it is estimated that up to 40,000 workers at one time were actively involved in moving iron, dirt or lumber. The magnitude of construction and the speed at which it progressed was a Fair Wonder all its own and the fair managers, always diligent as to possible sources of revenue, began charging .25 per person to view the construction and thousands were glad to pay it. The building process was also a dangerous one for the laborers with 18 fatalities in 1891 alone.*" So what to make of this quote? First it seems to be making Hermetic references, as the main Hermetic number is three. Here were 30 workmen, who first placed three picks into the earth, and all of the workmen were Italians (ie descendants of Ancient Rome). I present things like this for to get the bottom of this story requires every article and writing of the time period be scoured for what might be called "doublespeak language" and saying one thing while meaning another. Rome and Italy is going to referenced over and over again with the expositions.

The claim as to how such Fairs as this could be built so quickly was because they were built with cheap materials, mostly wood and a facing called staff (a type of plaster, cement, and fiber). This was supposedly invented in Paris to quickly build earlier expositions. The buildings were then painted white. "Many of the buildings included sculptural details and, to meet the Exposition's opening deadline, chief architect Burnham sought the help of Chicago Art Institute instructor Lorado Taft to help complete them. Taft's efforts included employed a group of talented women sculptors from the Institute known as "the White Rabbits" to finish some of the buildings, getting their name from Burnham's comment "Hire anyone, even white rabbits if they'll do the work." Recall the white rabbit is a key element to Alice in Wonderland and Through the Looking Glass. So again it is not just throw up a building cheap and quick, you have to add the fine sculptures, ornamentation, the grand towers and domes. And you really have to ask why. Why go to all that trouble when much more simple would have made the same impression on the people, and guarantee to get the job done.

Construction of Agricultural Building, Chicago

Granted there are photographs of the Fair construction happening. The article above states that people would pay 25 cents to watch it. Of course there are no references to exactly what the people paying the 25 cents to watch, and the photos that do exist are odd at times. Most of them show buildings at the entire base finished (like we see in the Agriculture Building below) with a layer of scaffolding along it. It might be indicating construction work, or more likely painting work. Sometimes there is work being done on a dome (sometimes construction, sometimes renovation). hat leads to the question. Was the building in fact built, or perhaps just the dome added to it. If it was an

60

original building did it have a different dome, and all that was done was to change domes? Another question with the photo above is the giant stack of wood planks. Is that is all the building materials needed on site, with no other sign of any construction tools, or workers, or carts, or cement making troughs, or anything. One horse, one guy and some wood. This type of photo will appear again and again, especially with the construction photos from St. Louis Exposition, where we have hundred of pictures that show the entire site from above, yet not even the stack of wood planks. Just scaffold completed buildings and no materials or workers anywhere around.

Construction of the Administration Building, with obvious parts of it penciled in.

Many of the "photos" that exist of the construction provide wide shots that in fact have much of the image added over or penciled in (such as the one of the Administration Building above). Parts of the front of the Building, like the lower scaffolding, are obviously penciled in.

Do I believe many of the buildings were temporary for this fair. Absolutely. I have found building photos from the 1897 Fair in Tennessee that very clearly show the buildings in a state of wood inner construction. There are similar photos in the White City documentary. But there are so many photos that tend to reveal original structures. The question is how many were temporary built structures that required a new building, and how many were already there (at least partially)and simply needed restoration? The no noise work? That is the question. Because one last telling feature to mention, is that so far, no one has been able to locate any blueprints for any of the fair buildings. Blueprints for many early buildings survive, but not one of building plans for anything at the Exposition.[32] The buildings seem to go up without problem in the two years, but then shortly after the fair began new building projects. Those did not go as smoothly, such as for the Coliseum.

Second Chicago Coliseum

Originally Chicago had Coliseum that held horse shows, boxing, and circus events starting in 1866. However there is no real documentation as to when this building was built, or even when it closed. Just that some 30 years later there was a need for new second Coliseum. It is important for our Exposition section because it was built in Woodlawn, on a part of the torn down Columbia Exposition. The construction began in 1895, one year after the fair ended, and was built on a 14-acre site. However on August 22, the building collapsed and had to be restarted. When complete it finished at 300 x 700 feet and 100 feet high using 2.5 million pounds of steel, 3.2 million feet of lumber, and 3 million bricks. This building is the size of one of the medium sized found at the Fair. Just a year or two later should have had the same workers and architects, now with the knowledge of having built 200 of these...yet this one collapses (obviously from poor construction methods). How can that be, when the work crews should be experts by now. It opened in July 1896 with a Buffalo Bill Wild West Show. That one

---

[32] It is sort of like NASA just "losing" all the original photos and video from the moon landing. Yes it is the most important event in the history of humans, but somehow they just got in the wrong box and thrown in the garbage. They were lost (hidden away) because too many people were starting see through the lies.

building took a full year to build, and when through at least one roof collapse (not from heavy snow but simple poor construction techniques). How did this fair get built in two years?

But they were not just building the fair. They needed to build some other magic buildings all over Chicago at the exact same time. Like they don't have enough to do to build 690 acres of buildings, they have to construct a few other Roman/Gothic-style monuments that will have nothing to do with the Exposition.

*

UNIVERSITY

Original building of the University of Chicago.

The University of Chicago is an oddity of history. It began in 1856 in the castle building above. While it can not be seen in this photo, the building is isolated from the city. A fort called Camp Douglas (a Civil War prisoner of war camp) was used for a while. Nothing else is around but empty space. Why would you build this castle in the middle of nowhere, to be a university? Then put a POW camp beside it? I have looked for information about the construction of this building, and of course have found nothing.

The university stuck around until 1886, when it supposedly ran into financial problems that came after a fire (with no mention of how it started) that seems to have burned down everything but the main tower. What is odd is that the sentence on Wikipedia of the fire claims, "In

1874, a fire damaged the university's main physical plant." What exactly is a physical plant, and why does a simple university building shaped like a castle need one? I have found photos of the demolition of the tower in 1890.[33]

They went out looking for financial support to rebuild, specifically to John Rockefeller. He refused. With that the university was forced to shut down. Stepping in was the same John Rockefeller who now changed the name to The Old University of Chicago, so that he could create a new university called The University of Chicago (financed by one John Rockefeller). A very sneaky trick to basically take the university all for himself. Then he could open where it is now (right next to the Columbian Exhibition Midway). Since that time all fairs have had a "midway" of carnival rides and activities. It is why Chicago University Football Club, located right next door the fair, became known as the original "Monsters of the Midway." Construction of the new buildings began in 1890, right as the World Fair is being set up next door at Jackson Park. Of course this new university has a number of Gothic buildings and cathedrals that might not look out of place in Tudor England. Just take a gander on Google Earth at all the old style buildings that make up Chicago University.

Does that not seem odd to you? To build this at the exact same time they were constructing the 690 acre Worlds Fair at Jackson Park- yet John Rockefeller can gather a workforce to build a university right next door. And then not use ANY of the university buildings for the Expo. The claim is that "the old campus left an affinity for Gothic architecture" hence the reason to build the new university as they did. This comment from Wikipedia is telling to our argument, "The university's current mascot of a Phoenix rising from the ashes is a reference to the fire, foreclosure, and demolition of the original Bronzeville campus with the current Hyde Park campus emerging triumphantly in its place. As an homage to this pre-1890 legacy a single stone from the rubble of the original Douglas Hall in Bronzeville was brought to the current Hyde Park location and set into the wall of the Classics Building...All told these connections have led the Dean of the College and University of Chicago and Professor of History John Boyer to conclude that the University of Chicago has a "plausible genealogy as a pre– Civil War institution."[34]

---

[33] Photos of the building can be found here, including some of its demolition in 1890
   http://photoarchive.lib.uchicago.edu/db.xqy?show=browse2.xml|176
[34] Found in John Boyer, The University of Chicago: A History.

This is another sly comment, claiming from one saved stone that the University is much older. I think it the way of saying that the university buildings are much older. That these buildings must have been there before the fair. I mean can you really divert manpower from building a 690 acre site, that has less than two years to finish and has today's equivalent of a billion dollars invested in its construction?

Chicago Cultural Center. Notice the amazing dome topped skyscraper in the background.

I have already mentioned the very odd City Hall in town. And if you go two blocks over you come to the Chicago Cultural Center (originally the Public Library), and its special Preston Bradley Hall. It also looks right out of a Rome or Greece handbook. And when did it begin to be built...ah yes you guessed it, 1893 during the World's Fair. Does not everyone in Chicago have enough to do with the Exposition? No, they need to build this (because you know why not). What is most magnificent is what is inside it.

Preston Bradley Hall is a giant round room, full of mosaics and made of white Carrara marble. At its center is a 38-foot Tiffany glass dome, the largest Tiffany dome in the world. According to the site atlasobscura dot com, it has 1,134 square feet of colored mosaics, 30,000 individual panes of glass, and is valued at $35,000,000. Those are the signs of the zodiac moving around the dome which resembles the scales of a fish (which is a symbol of the ruling elite). I wish I had a better photo, the only one now is the one you see which is a public domain photo, but if you google this you can get even more impressive views of this dome and room. Who needs to build this DURING the World's Exposition?

Just for fun, open up Google Earth and go for a little Chicago trip. Start at City Hall- with the Tower across the street, over to the Cultural Center- and opposite is Millennium Park. Check out the beautiful curved column structure at the head of what is obviously a very specific geometric layout of the park. Follow along and you come to an odd Sphere (that may represent the Black Sun) is in the middle of the park. It is called the Cloud Gate, built in 2006 and is 33 feet high and 66 feet wide and with the length of the arch creates a phi relationship of the structure.[35]

Field Museum opening 1921

Follow that down you come to the Field Museum (built in 1911 to house the Columbian exhibits moved from the Palace of Fine Arts). The photo above is opening day in 1921. As you can see it is built in the middle of nowhere. Granted Soldier Field (that looked like the Circus Maximus) would be built next to it shortly. Actually it is a shame the modern renovation happened in 2002, for now the ancient look of Soldier Field is mostly gone. You can only see it in photos of the 1920's and 30's. But this is about the Field Museum, for here is a photo of its supposed construction.

---

[35] from youtube Sacred Geometry Decoded channel

Field Museum 1921

What we are seeing here is the similar construction photos we are going to see from all the fairs. A complete building, photographed with a few pieces of scaffolding around it and no other sign that this is a building site other than it is surrounded by mud. This question will be asked again is this a photo of a construction site, or a site that has been dug out of the mud then refurbished and repainted?

So what is the true history of this city then? In fact a question to ask is what is history itself. Who was writing the history of the United States. Of course it becomes no surprise to find that the main person who wrote the entire history of the USA was also the same man who wrote the book of the history of the Columbian Exhibition.

*

HUGH BANCROFT

HH Bancroft

" Of all the pleasant features connected with the Fair, one of the most pleasant was the appreciation, we might almost say the affection with which it was regarded. While the greatest international exposition that the world ever witnessed has passed into history, it has bequeathed a heritage for good which cannot readily be estimated, shedding a flood of light on millions of lives and filling the land with the sunshine of beauty and truth."
HH Bancroft

We have to look very closely at the man who wrote *The Book of the Fair*, both figuratively and literally. Because he is just as important as the book, and from the standpoint of the history of the US, he might BE the history of the USA. I did not give you the complete title of his Chicago Exposition book which is,*"The Book of the Fair: Designed to set forth the display made by the Congress of Nations, of human achievement in material form, so as the more effectually to illustrate the progress of mankind in all departments of civilized life"* by Hubert Howe Bancroft. That was the title of the book. Like just how pretentious can you get? So just who is this guy?

Well, he was born in 1832 in Ohio and became the man who wrote the first history of The Western USA, Texas, California, British Columbia, Mexico and Native Indians. After finishing his schooling he went to become a clerk in the bookstore of his brother-in-law in Buffalo. "In March 1852, Bancroft was provided with an inventory of books to sell and was sent to the booming California city of San Francisco to set up a West Coast regional office of the firm. Bancroft was successful in building his company, entering the world of publishing in the process."[36] In 1852 he was sent to San Francisco to sell books! As we have seen, San Francisco was supposed to have only been founded in 1847 two years before the gold rush. The only people there should be cowboys and miners. How many of them could even read? So who was he selling books to?

"He also became a serious collector of books, maps, and manuscript documents building a collection numbering into the tens of thousands of volumes including a large number of narratives dictated to Bancroft or his assistants by pioneers, settlers, and statesmen. The indexing of the vast collection employed six persons for ten years. The

[36]Wikipedia according to *Men and Women of America: A Biographical Dictionary of Contemporaries.* New York: L.R. Hamersly and Co., 1910; p. 87

library was moved in 1881 to a fireproof building and, in 1900, numbered about 45,000 volumes." A collection of 60,000 books was later purchased by Berkeley University and placed in its named Bancroft Library. He left business after The Civil War to devote himself entirely to writing and publishing history.[37] Collector is the key word here. I believe that is what he was doing out west. I think the going to California to sell books is a smoke screen. He was sent there to collect every document from the area (perhaps from the early cities that had just been located).

I believe that he used the found "ancient" books, manuscripts and maps that had come into his possession to know much of the complete early history of the Americas. But if he wanted to present that real history, he only would have had to update and republish what he had discovered. He could have just reprinted the found books. But my guess is that he did not present the real history, but did the same thing the Egyptologists of Egypt do. Anything important that is found is locked away in the Cairo Museum and never mentioned or seen again. My guess here is that Bancroft did the same, by turning over key documents to the Smithsonian for "safe keeping" (which means to be put into a safe so no one can ever see them). He then sent to work, with a group of 600 collaborators[38] to create the "new history" of North and South America. That is how important this man might be, he could literally be the creator of all we know of as the history of North and South America. He was the one who wrote close to 10,000 pages on the history of the Native peoples, and was the source for decades that all anthropologists used for their studies. Which is why his book of the Chicago Fair is so important, for he may not just be presenting what turns out to be a very valuable catalog of all the buildings and exhibits, but perhaps the culmination of the very historical ideas he himself originally created.

He wrote 39 volumes each about 1500 pages long. That is over 60,000 pages.. But one has to ask, how can one man write 39 books of 1500 pages each in less than 20 years by himself? Well the same way the great Chicago Exposition was supposed to be built in 2 years. It can't. He had a lot of help to write it, and most of it went through unchecked (the volumes are full of grammatical and spelling errors). Even during his lifetime he was under scrutiny for his work. The Salt Lake Tribune called him a "purloiner of other peoples' brains" in 1893.

[37] Wilson, J. G.; Fiske, J., eds. (1900). "Bancroft, Hubert Howe" . Wilson, J. G.; Fiske, J., eds. (1900). "Bancroft, Hubert Howe" . Appletons' Cyclopædia of American Biography. New York: D. Appleton
[38] Encyclopedia Britannica

Oregon historian William Alfred Morris presented an essay on Bancroft in the Oregon History Quarterly where he presents that most of what Bancroft claimed as his own was actually written by others. "This tainted his legacy in the eyes of some scholars, on the principle "false in one thing, false in all."[39] This does not taint his eyes to me, it more showcases just how much of a fraud his historical work must be.

In the final chapter of his Fair book he presents the wonderful library at Berkeley (that has all his source material) and presents a story of how he obtained all of them. "Nearly half a century of time and over half a million of dollars were consumed in making this collection. First, all the nooks and corners of North and Central and South American and the West India islands were searched for whatever had been written or printed therein, and whatever related to them which had been elsewhere published. Then Europe was several times visited in like manner; and in numberless instances where the desired books and manuscripts could not be purchased, copies were made. Work of this kind was done in all the great libraries of England, France, and Germany, of Italy and Spain. Everything in St. Petersburg relating to Alaska was translated and copied...The archives of Spain and Mexico supplied masses of historic data relating to the conquest and occupation of Spanish America, while chronicles of the doings of Anglo-Americans on the western slope were secured in the older settled sections of the eastern side." Another question to ask, is just who financed the half million dollars that he claims it took to do all the cataloging. There is never mention of where the money was obtained.

While I do not believe the historical record he presents, I do feel the study of his books is important for I do believe that his collection research got him the documents that revealed the true history of North and South America. I think he knew the truth, preserved it for his freemasonic elite friends, then wrote what was going to be the narrative that they wanted the common people (us) to believe. And most of us have, until the very recent time. So again his book of the fair for me is beyond important, and when this project is complete I am going to back and read through some of his other books, for I feel he he may have found the truth of America's origins- and like any author, it will sneak into his writing.

---

[39] Morris, William Alfred (1903). "The Origin and Authorship of the Bancroft Pacific States Publications: A History of a History (part 1)" . Oregon Historical Quarterly. Vol. 4.

I have come across a glorious old book, and one that might have been one of the many that Bancroft had found originally. Today it can be found uploaded from the Internet, *America: Being the latest and most accurate description of the New World* by John Ogilby in 1671. It is to be found in the Smithsonian Library, which again gives credence to me that they got what Bancroft found. This book, if you read very closely, presents that the inhabitants of North America's West at this time had cities of over 30,000 people, who lived in four-story lime and stone houses. Four story buildings! Where are these buildings? Who was living in them? The depictions of many things in the book are spot on, so this is claiming civilization in North America beyond tepees and wigwams.

Why do I say he wrote the history to please his freemasonic friends? In one early chapter on the history of Chicago in *The Book Of The Fair*, he mentions how Chicago has built wonderful architecture in the city. He gives the reader a tour of just one of those buildings, which is the Masonic Temple Building. He mentions no other, but goes into detail of the building itself. Especially the upper freemasonic lodge. That can be no clearer a message than can be sent. Bancroft is a freemason, writing the history that freemasons want presented to the masses. We have to recognize that if we are ever going to get to the truth of history. [40]

*

WHAT IS CHICAGO?

But the point of this chapter was to present that everywhere you turn in Chicago with anything claimed to be built before 1930, looks like you are in Ancient Rome or Central Europe. I think this the point. Chicago is Rome, or is meant to portray it. It seems the Columbian Exhibition of 1893 was the centerpiece of this entire odd city.

Why create a fair from scratch and make it look like Ancient Rome? I mean this is Chicago 1893, the start of the skyscraper bonanza. If the fair is all about showing off modern technological progress, and especially American progress- why make all the fair look like you were in Ancient Rome or Greece? Why not show off the new American city building craze? I think there is a very important reason for this. They wanted to symbolize that America was the new Rome in the

---

[40] He is not alone. The others of the time period who were the main historical writers of standard history, were also writing the story of the Exposition (such as JW Buel for St. Louis in 1904).

world, the center of everything. Or even to show that Chicago was Rome, or a second Rome. When I looked at the latitude of Chicago it lays at 41 50 north. You will find that this is the exact same from Rome. In fact St Peters Basilica is almost at the exact same latitude as Chicago's City Hall. When you follow that line around the globe, no other major city falls along it. Just Chicago and Rome.

Whether Chicago was an eastern city in the old Roman Empire is hard to prove at this point. It is very possible that Roman-Greek style buildings existed in North America before the European arrival in the 1500's or whenever they finally arrived (maybe not even until 1776). The cities then seem to be added to, to present the USA as the new Roman Empire. The Expositions were no exception. In fact I believe they chose a very specific Roman location to be their model for the Fair (as I will describe in the chapter 8). Again Chicago is by no means unique historically, as we will see in the upcoming chapters of the other cities (really look at the history of San Francisco when we come to it.

For now we move to the 700 acre Chicago Columbian Exhibition. The first point is, we are not even now sure what the word Columbian is referring to!

CHAPTER 4
THE COLUMBIAN EXPOSITION 1893

Chicago's White City 1893, or Ancient Rome?

To the Chicago Exhibition itself, where the photos reveal the grandeur of Ancient Rome in its heyday. I suggest to watch the excellent 2005 documentary called *Expo-White City,* to get a sense of just how giant of an exhibition this was. You could have been at this event for days and not come close to seeing all of it. I still use Bancroft's book as a reference, but there are so many others, some of them actual guide books from 1893, exactly like Lonely Planets of today. One is *A Week at The Fair: Illustrating Exhibits and Wonders* put out by Rand McNally. Yes that Rand McNally. It is a 500 page guide of every building, every entrance fee, every exhibit, every place to eat and drink. Other good sources are the books *the Photographic History of the World Fair* and *Sketch of the City of Chicago* by James Wilson Pierce (which is great for showing drawings of the great architecture of the city), *Plans and Diagrams of All Exhibit Buildings In The World Columbian Exhibition,* and *Shepps Worlds Fair Photographed.*

Speaking of photographs, at the Columbia Exhibition it was forbidden to take any photos unless one paid a two dollar fee. That was a massive charge at the time, and as such almost no one took any. Special police walked the event just to try and arrest people for taking photos. I searched the photos of the fair that do exist to see if I could notice anyone walking around with something that looked like photographic equipment. I could find no one. As such all the photos that have come from the fair are generally from CD Arnold and William Henry Jackson.[41] Why did they not want anyone to take photographs?

*

THE WHITE CITY

The exposition covered 690 acres (2.8 km2), had 200 giant buildings (again all supposedly temporary) along with canals and lagoons. More than 27 million people attended the exposition during its six-month run. There was only 62 million in the entire US at the time. Granted many would be repeat visitors, but still, where did all these people come from? And why were many fairgoers given things that seem like modern passports as their entrance? Without an Eiffel Tower like Paris, Chicago's new entrant was the first Ferris Wheel, and a long parade of entertainment called the Midway.[42] The Exposition was an inspiration for many, including the author of Wizard of Oz, L Frank Baum who modeled his Emerald City after the Chicago Expo. The fair opened on May 1 and closed October 31.[43] It was supposed to open in 1892 to celebrate the 400 th anniversary of Christopher Columbus's voyage, but the "slow" building process pushed it back a year. Oddly the fair was still "officially opened" October 21 1892 with something very strange. They had one hundred young schoolchildren reciting, for the first time, the Pledge of Allegiance, lined up in what Wikipedia calls "military fashion." The Pledge was written by Francis J. Bellamy "specifically to bring national attention to the fair and the first national Columbus Day holiday." Thus the US Pledge of Allegiance is actually tied to this Fair, the lie of Columbus, and all the symbolism that he stands for. There would be no closing ceremony in October 1893, as just days prior Chicago's mayor was assassinated at his home by a man supposedly

---

[41] Jackson was a famous early photographer of the American West. He is great-nephew of Samuel Wilson, the man who originated the Uncle Sam image.

[42] The Best source to look at around 1000 photos of the fair is the 1893 book Shepps World Fair Photographs found at internet site
https://archive.org/details/worldsfairphoto00sheprich

[43] Illuminati dates of its founding and Halloween.

upset for not getting an exposition job. In as sense this Fair opened and closed with two odd ceremonies, the children doing the Pledge of Allegiance, and at the other end a political assassination.

Referring to the Fair as The White City got a lot of people upset, for many felt it was not really a nickname to describe the fair, but the "ideas behind the fair." Almost immediately black activists claimed that there were no African American exhibits or influence in any area. Frederick Douglass, Ida B. Wells, Irvine Garland Penn, and Ferdinand Lee Barnett coauthored a pamphlet entitled "The Reason Why the Colored American is not in the World's Columbian Exposition." Eventually some blacks were included in small ways- a sculptor or painting exhibit. At this time racism and segregation in the US, particularly the south, was rising to new levels, which had been lessened at the end of Civil War.[44]

*

COLUMBIA

65 foot high Statue of the Republic, who is Columbia-Liberty-Isis

---

[44] One note, a internet researcher of these topics presented that the capitals of this ancient civilization were called "White Cities." To her cites such as Prague, Paris, Nantes, Rome, Moscow, Washington, London, and Chicago were all White Cites- so named due to the style and colour of the stone used in their architecture. Thus to her the naming of the Exposition as a White City, could also have been a reference to its original function before the new European arrival. To date hers is the only such reference to this hypotheses, but I present it simply as something to ponder.

75

In the middle of the Great Court was the 65 foot tall Statue of the Republic. It was given the nickname "The Golden Lady." Most believe it was covered with gold leaf, but some speculate it might have been made out of solid gold. Made by Daniel French, who used Edith Stokes as his model, the statue stood at the Casino end of the Great Basin, looking towards the Administration Building. The statue's right hand holds an orb, while an eagle with wings spread (Horus) perched on it. The other hand held a staff with a winding serpent and a plaque with the word "liberty" partly obscured by an encircling laurel wreath. The original gold did not appear on any of the exposed skin of the statue (head, neck or arms). The statue survived two of the fires at the fair, but not the third in 1896. A one-third size replica was made in 1918 out of bronze and can be found today in Jackson Park. This new small version is completely gilded, thus no exposed non golden skin, and the Phrygian cap is not on top of the staff, but draped over it. Why exactly they did not want to make an exact replica is beyond me. I think many people today are fooled thinking the current statue is the original from the fair. What did the original Golden Lady represent? The Statue of the Republic was a Statue of Columbia, of Isis and the Statue of Liberty all in one. Who was Columbia?

The exposition went by the name Columbian. The name is presented as a way honor Christoper Columbus the explorer. But the name was not the Columbus Exposition, but the Columbian Exposition. The word Columbia is claimed to have derived in the 1700's out of Christopher Columbus, adding an ia to end. The word has appeared all over the US. The capital of the country is in the District of Columbia (which is not a state and technically not in the US), Columbia University, or the Columbia River.

Columbia

Columbia is not an explorer, she is a mythical female figure, wearing an American flag and a Phrygian cap, which signified freedom and the pursuit of liberty. She is the American version of Isis. "Columbia is the personification of the United States," and the name "has occasionally been proposed as an alternative word for American." Thus now Columbian Exposition can mean American Exposition, or the Exposition of the mystical figure of the Americas. A second related controversial idea is that the Statue of Liberty in New York has always been in the United States. Where it is placed today, on so named Liberty Island, she sits on top of a giant "very weathered" square base, which sits inside of a star fort. The Statue of Liberty was originally perceived as the personification of Columbia as Lady Liberty. The Statue was supposed to have been made in France and sent to the US as a gift in the 1880's. We do have a few photos of it in France, and photos of the statue in NY City. If the statue is the personification of America, then why would the French make it and send it. It is more likely it was made in the USA.[45]

In 1863 a female Statue of Freedom was placed atop the United States Capitol Building. A similar statue was placed above the Memorial

---

[45] Another has suggested that the Statue of Liberty was originally the great statue at either Rhodes or Alexandria.

Hall at the 1876 Philadelphia Exhibition. And yes, the giant golden female statue at the Chicago Exposition in 1893, was fully known by the patrons (though called officially The Statue of the Republic) to be Columbia. One last item, in case there is any question that the Statue of Liberty is Columbia. Look at the start of any Columbia Motion Picture. The statue is right in the center, with only the word Columbia (not Columbia Pictures) and then there is a zoom in to the light of the torch. The Statue of Liberty is a Statue of Columbia, and the statue of the Chicago World Exhibition is Columbia. By keeping that in mind more of what was going one here may reveal itself.

*

THE BUILDINGS

While there is lots to explore and present on this fair, we should begin with what hits most in the photographs, the giant gleaming white buildings. I will not provide the detail of every building and area of the exposition, there are many books that do just that. Here I will give a basic overview and some of the elements that cause us to ask further questions. So big was the fair, doctors actually gave advice to people as to how to attend it. Doctor Hillmantel suggested, "*Come to the Fair early; avoid exposure to the sun; keep quiet during the heat of the day, and on hot days explore only a limited area. Don't loiter or saunter, but move rapidly from point to point; when examining an exhibit stand still and take it in with the eyes and not with the feet; for nothing is more fatiguing than the constant shifting of the body's weight from one foot to another.*"[46]

---

[46]Both quotes from Bancrofts Fair book

Court of Honor

There were fourteen "great buildings" mostly surrounding a giant lake. This area was known as the Court of Honor. It was simply breathtaking. At one end was a colonnade known as the peristyle. Three fountains were at the other end, representing the ships of Columbus.

The Massive Manufacture and Liberal Arts Building

The most magnificent was the Manufacturers and Liberal Arts Building. The Chicago Tribune remarked in 1893, "Without underrating the vast treasures of human industry and art that are collected at Jackson Park, the buildings themselves are the greatest attraction. For vast extent, boldness of conception, wonderful engineering, faultless proportions, and impressive grandeur the Manufactures building is easily the greatest of them all." It was not just the biggest building at the fair, but the biggest at the time on the Earth. It was 1650 feet long (almost 6 football fields) and covered 30 acres. At the center it rose to a height of 200 feet, half the height of the Great Pyramid. The roof was supported on gigantic steel trusses, which spanned the entire width. Eight domes were found on either side of 80 feet high entrance ways. Externals of the building were in the Corinthian style of architecture with many columns and arches. It was ornamented with female statues, to symbolize the arts and sciences. There were four entrances at the center of each side, being 10 feet wide and 80 feet high. On top of each was an 18 foot tall eagle. Outside, the building was lit by 10,000 electric lights, suggested by some to be more than existed in all of New York City at the time.

Initial concert with 100,000 guests in October, 1892

Chicagology claimed the building was four times as large as the Roman Colosseum, which seated eighty thousand people. At the opening ceremony in 1892 picture above, a concert was held, and 100,000 people were easily accommodated. In fact organizers speculated that they could fit 300,000 people into the building. Grasp your head around the size of that. The Rose Bowl in Pasadena today holds 100,000 people for football games, yet this "temporary building" of wood, iron and plaster staff could hold 300,000.

Inside were thousands of exhibits from countries all over the world. Just about any product anyone could think of (chemical products, pharmaceuticals, dyes, upholstery, china, jewelry, glassware, stoves, musical instruments, medical supplies, silver, gold, books, scientific instruments and various kinds of art) could be found there. Six massive football fields full of everything from everywhere. The long half mile walkway in the middle was known as Columbia Avenue, who at its center had a giant clock tower that rang ever hour.

Agricultural Building

The Agricultural Hall was built in the style of the Renaissance and was 500 by 850 feet. On each side of the entrance were 50 feet high Corinthian pillars. A 100 foot rotunda was covered by a 130 feet high glass dome. It housed exhibits of agriculture, forestry, dairy, and livestock and included amphitheaters, lecture halls and a dairy school. The Machinery Hall (image in chapter 2) was filled with giant towers, beautiful columns and view over the canal. It mirrored the style of the Spanish Renaissance and had a size at 500 by 1,350 feet which covered seventeen acres. Inside was nearly every kind of machine imaginable. The problem was, that with all of the working all the time, it was just too loud for anyone to be inside the building, and that included the people supposed to be in there working them. The Horticultural Building was 1,000 feet long and faced the lagoon. The center pavilion was roofed by a crystal dome 187 feet in diameter and 11 feet high, to have space for the large trees and palms that the building displayed. At each end of the building were cafes (which like the rest of the fair served very overpriced food and drink). The Fish and Fisheries Building was 1,100 feet long and exhibited all that one could imagine of the fish industry, including one the first great aquariums (totaling 14,000 gallons of water) where people could see fish, sharks and the like up close for the first time.

Government Building behind the Wooded Island

But there was far more. The Government Building was also massive. Made to look like a copy of the Capitol in Washington, it was 350 by 420 feet. A central octagonal dome 120 feet in diameter and 150 feet high stood at the middle. To include the listing from Bancroft's book of every exhibit in the building would have taken up 20 pages, to give you a sample of just how much each and every one of these buildings contained. The Transportation Building was 960 by 250 feet, with the interior modeled after a Roman basilica. Three sections of the building displayed railroads, shipping and vehicle exhibits. There was an entire section just for bicycles. Eight elevators could take people to the top of the 165 foot high dome for views of the fairgrounds. The entrance to the building was through a giant golden door. The Woman's Building was 400 feet long, and included a rotunda, and an giant skylight, surrounded by a two-story open arcade, giving the appearance of an Italian Renaissance court yard. This building could only display objects: painting, sculpture, or writing that were created by women (or in the case of textiles) only for women. Opposite the Machinery Hall and in the center of the grand plaza was the Administration building, with a statue of Columbus at the entrance. A central rotunda rose its gilded dome to a height of 275 feet above the grounds, and resembling somewhat the dome of the Invalids in Paris.

Electricity was a major part of the fair. There was a war to see who would gain the electricity rights, between General Electric Company (backed by Thomas Edison and J.P. Morgan) and Westinghouse (using Nikola Tesla's alternating current system). Westinghouse won out, but not with bitter feelings between the two (they both tried to ban the other's products from use at the fair). Tesla was considered a mad scientist, but that is only because he may have fully understood the ancient way of generating and using power (used in all the Medieval structures), idea that the "current" "power"ful elite wanted hidden from humanity.[47] In the center of the building, and forming a part of the exhibits of the General Electric company, was the Edison tower (tower of light) with thousands of miniature lamps arranged in crystal. It would be like a forerunner to the main building 20 years later (Tower of Jewels) at the 1915 San Francisco Fair. Along with the electrical displays were Thomas Edison's kinetoscope, search lights, a seismograph, switchboard, electric incubators for chicken eggs, and Morse code telegraph. One of Tesla's many exhibits was called the "Egg of Columbus," a metal egg that spun on a disk to demonstrate a rotating magnetic field.

The electrical building was the only one at the fair (along with the Machinery Building) with giant towers around it. The first question is why? Many of the Fair buildings have domes, but only the Electrical and Machinery Buildings had towers. So why the two buildings that need the most electricity have the towers? I think many researchers have it correct. Towers and domes are a part of the ancient system of creating free energy from the atmosphere. It is possible that the Electrical Building was not just a place to house all the electrical exhibits, but was in fact an energy generating power station on its own.

---

[47] Tesla eventually died impoverished on 7 January 1943. His tesla coils, towers and other devices have been shown to create free energy directly from the atmosphere. He had been working on a time travel device, and on his death, the man who took charge of all of Tesla's inventions was a electrical engineer at MIT- John Trump, yes the nephew of Donald. That part is true. Added to it are conspiracy rumors that speculates that the Trump family continued the work of Tesla in the field of time travel, and it was this work that allowed Donald to become US President.

Palace of Fine Arts

The Palace of Fine Arts is one of the only seven structures still standing today[48] (and is now the Museum of Science and Industry). It exhibited some of the finest painting, sculpture and statuary in four great courts. The Chicago Tribune wrote of the building "The style of architecture adapted in the building was of the Grecian-Ionic order and the blending and adaptation of what was most perfect in the past was such as to secure an effect, if not in the exact sense original, at least of great harmony and grandeur." Around 50 feet high, and resting on a basement raised nine feet above ground, the building is 320 by 500 feet and covers an area of nearly five acres. At the middle is a giant rotunda 125 feet high along with a dome.

---

[48]- The second building still in Chicago is the World's Congress Building (one of the few buildings not built in Jackson Park, instead it was built downtown in Grant Park). The Maine State building is now in Portland Mass., The Dutch Cocao House (a copy of Franeker City Hall) was moved brick by brick and is now an apartment in Brookline Mass. The Pabst Beer Pavilion moved to the Pabst mansion (and when given over the local Catholic church to became a private chapel for the Archbishop), The Norway Pavilion (a Stave Kirke) was moved to Illinois, then back to Norway in 2015. The final remaining structure is a ticket both. This according to the site Digital Research Library of Illinois

Palace of fine arts in 1924.

The reason the Palace still exists today is because it was supposed to have been built with a brick substructure under its plaster facade. To get insurance for all the artwork the building had to be fire proof. But why only put brick in this one building? And why only the art in this building needed insurance? Were there not priceless artifacts all over the Expo? There are photos of the building much late, as the one above in 1924. It does look to be in rather bad state of being in 1924 when the photo was taken...but is is from being a temporary structure, or from being so old.

*

STATE AND COUNTRY

Illinois Building

There was far far more at this Fair. Each of the 48 states in the union had their own building. Some were rather simple, some were elaborate. On one side of the lagoon was Illinois building. Made in the shape of a Greek cross it was 450 feet long by 160 feet wide, and of course include a 152 foot high dome. The California building was 435 by 115 feet, built to look like the old Mission Church of San Diego, which included its main tower. Here they displayed all the fresh California produce available, as a way of promoting their state as "the best place to live in the US." The Pennsylvania building was of the colonial style of architecture, and reproduced the historic clock-tower with its Liberty Bell. Yes there was a replica of the Liberty Bell here for the Exposition. Oddly the replica bell seems to have wound up in Russia at the start of the 1917 Bolshevik Revolution. What is most odd is the claims at the time that the state buildings were all constructed of marble. Permanent buildings, the reason having been given was each state wanted to show the others "how great their state was." This information tends not to appear in current books or documentaries about the fair, because you have to start asking when you know that, why build state buildings out of marble (but not the rest). Why tear down buildings built of marble, when that would be a very difficult and time consuming job. Secondly they could have been used for many functions afterward, as was the "only permanent building" the Palace of Fine Arts. My feeling is that this is a "glitch" in the story...one that is usually glossed over but should not be. The state buildings are said clearly to have been built as permanent stone structures, yet they too came down with the rest. So what is the true story?

Close to 100 countries had buildings as well. France built a recreation of the Palace of Versailles, Germany a reconstruction of a Bavarian town hall, while Japan had a beautiful pavilion on the Wooded Island of flowers and trees. Every country came to showcase its art, products and country. Famed German arms manufacturer Krupp also had a massive building to showcase its guns and artillery. It was basically a showcase of what would be used in twenty years time during the First World War.

Norway's Viking Ship

Norway had a very unique exhibit at the fair, the Viking Ship. However, it was likely not so enjoyed by the fair organizers. Recall this was a fair to honor the story of Christopher Columbus and how his "discovery" of America made him the first European on the continent, and thus the start of "real history." If there was a before Columbus it would throw off the entire myth being created. The Norwegians had long known that their Vikings had been in the Americas around 1000AD, if not far earlier. Thus Norway built a replica of a Viking ship, and had it sailed across the Atlantic (another shot in the historical arm, proving such ships could make the journey) all the way to the Chicago Fair. The "Viking," was 76 feet long, a single sail, and rigged with oars. It was captained by Magnus Andersen. The Viking ship stayed in North

America after the fair, Lincoln Park first, and then after 1996 to Geneva, Illinois.[49]

*

MIDWAY

World's Original Ferris Wheel

A long stretch of open space away from the main buildings became known as the Midway. While the main fair was to promote art, culture, architecture, and technology, the midway was about vice. Beer, food, dancing girls, exotic exhibits, and music. It became the main attraction of the fair where visitors spent much of their time. The "Street in Cairo" exhibit was extremely popular and made to be like a giant Egypt bazaar. Here you could get Middle Eastern food, smoke a hookah, see a dancer known as Little Egypt who is claimed to have been the first to dance a very sensual belly dance later called the "hootchy-kootchy." But there was a Moroccan Village, Irish Village, German Village, Italian Square. It was as if a small piece of everywhere on earth had a plot on the Midway.

The main attraction on the Midway was a new one to the world, the Ferris Wheel. Designed by George Washington Gale Ferris it was much much larger than what we are used to today. Fair organizers

---

[49] Interesting Norway also had one one of the only buildings to survive the fair, a copy of a Stave Kirke (wood church) it sent overseas. After the fair it was moved to Little Norway, Wisconsin, then was sent back to Norway in 2015 and now is in Orkdal, just outside of Trondheim.

wanted a landmark to match the Eiffel Tower in Paris, and this was as rival. Basically it was designed like a giant bicycle wheel. Its top height was a massive 250 feet in the air. It held 36 cars, each carrying 40 passengers, which meant 1,440 people would ride the giant wheel at the same time. Over 3 million people rode the wheel at the fair, turning in a great profit. However this great monument did not last like the Tower in Paris did. It stayed in Chicago a short while, then was used at the 1904 Exposition in St. Louis. In 1906 it was destroyed and sold for scrap.

Then there were the anthropological exhibits, natives from all over the world. Eskimos with their mush dogs, Penobscot wigwams, a village of supposed cannibals from Africa, the Cliff Dwellers featured a rock and timber structure that was painted to recreate American Indian cliff dwellings of Colorado. Basically they were all set up as a human zoo where white fiargoers could see who they "evolved" from. One anthropology exhibit had lab assistants take measurements of fairgoers, who could then see how they measured up to statues representing the ideal image of the Anglo-Saxon man and woman. This was continued at future fairs.

Along the lakeside was the first moving walkway or travelator. It was designed so that people could get off their boats at the end of the pier and not have to walk to the casino (where the first cafes were found). It had two different segments, one where passengers were seated, and one where riders could stand or walk. However this great new innovation soon broke down and for most of the fair was never working. Eadweard Muybridge gave a series of lectures in the Zoopraxographical Hall, which was basically the first place to show moving pictures to the public. Several products that are well known today were first introduced at the Exposition including Juicy Fruit Gum, Cream of Wheat, Pabst Blue Ribbon beer, the Brownie, and Quaker Oats. Scott Joplin from Texarkana played his piano, John Philip Sousa's Band presented concerts, and it was the first time the Mormon Tabernacle Choir appeared outside of Utah. However the large concerts were not well attended, given that so much exotic music from all over the world was free every day on the Midway.

*

CONGRESS

What were called The Congresses were very popular. They were not held at the fair grounds per sey, but in a building at Grant Park with seating for 3,000 people. They were basically two or three week long lecture sessions each on a special subject such as, finance, health, women's issues, railroads, history, folklore, science, philosophy, peace, psychology or religion. The first series to open was on Women's Progress on May 15, 1893.

The segment that has gained the most notoriety was called The Parliament of the World's Religions[50], that ran from September 11 to September 27. It is claimed to be the first gathering of representatives of all the major religious traditions from the West and East. Here one could hear not just Christian lectures, but Buddhist, Taoist, Islamic, or Hindu. For most Americans it would be the first time these Non-Christian religions could have been encountered. Doctor Barrows remarked, "Its (religion) great part in human history can be impressively told; its achievements can be narrated; its vast influence over art, ethics, education, liberty can be set forth; its present condition can be indicated; its missionary activities can be described, and best of all the spirit of mutual love, of cosmopolitan fraternity can be disclosed and augmented."

While most of the speeches were about the wonders of following their own faith, some used it as a platform to attack the present world order such as one Hindu monk who claimed, "We have been told to accept Christianity," he said, "because Christian nations are prosperous. We look at England, the richest Christian nation of the world. Why is she rich and prosperous? Because she has her foot upon the neck of 250,000,000 Asiatics. We read history and we see everywhere that Christianity has conquered prosperity by cutting the throats of its followers. At such a price the Hindu will have none of it."

A very interesting speaker, who I would have loved to have heard, was Mary C. Collins, called Winona by the Sioux Indians, among whom she has lived for many years with Sitting Bull on the prairie. "She stated that she had gone back and forth among them by day and night without meeting with a discourteous word or look, claiming for the Sioux a nobility of character which the world does not seem willing to accord."

---

[50]Quotes in this section come from Bancroft's book.

*

FIRES

After the January 1894 fire, Statue of Republic still in place as is much of the fairgrounds

No Worlds Fair can be complete without fires destroying many of the buildings, and Chicago is no exception. The first fire took place during the fair in the Cold Storage Building July 17, 1893. This building was basically a giant refrigerator to keep cold all of the meat that was being used in the fair's restaurants. It was so large that the middle was able to be turned into a giant skating rink, perhaps the first such indoor rink in the world. The building required a 200-foot iron chimney to run the refrigeration units, but designers believed that the smokestack would clash with the fair's other buildings. To remedy this, a wooden tower topped with a decorative cupola was built around the chimney. That made it a fire hazard.

When the fire broke out that was quickly put out by fire fighters. July 10 a new fire, much larger, broke out. Twenty firefighters responded. Due to the great amount of smoke they were forced to climb to the top of the tower and became trapped. With no other option as the tower was seconds away from burning down, a few were able to slide down burning fire hoses and ropes safely. Thirteen remained trapped, and most jumped to their deaths (in front of the thousands of witnesses of the fair). An estimated 50,000 fairgoers witnessed the fire, some with

91

a bird's-eye view from the top of the Ferris wheel. Initially the crowd was cheering on the firefighters, but they soon fell silent as they jumped. The fire department later reported, "never was so terrible a tragedy witnessed by such a sea of agonized faces."

The second fire came in January 1894, three months after the Fair had ended. Thousands may have witnessed this fire as well, at least it seems that way from the standard historical sources. However Bancroft's book lists two fires happening in 1894, this one in January and another in June. I have found no other source that presents there being two fires, only the one in January. What Bancroft provides as info for two fires, gets combined by history to one event. What does seem certain is that in January basically the entire Court of Honor and many of the buildings around it went up in flames. The fire started in the Casino, destroyed that building, then swept northward along the Peristyle into Music Hall. From there it ran across and into the Manufactures building. "For three hours the flames raged along the past end of the Court of Honor until nothing was left but charred timbers and blackened plaster. A shower of sparks fell upon the ice in the lagoon until it looked like a sea of fire; they fell upon the adjacent buildings, threatening them with destruction. It was a magnificent spectacle that drew ceaseless exclamations of wonder and awe from the spectators that crowded the grounds in the vicinity of the fire. It was the greatest pyrotechnic display of the Fair."[51] The cause of the blaze were claimed to be tramps, who had been hanging around the fair after it has closed down.

Bizarrely this is what the Chicago Tribune wrote "*trains were loaded down with throngs of excited people on their way to witness the great conflagration. They poured through the gate of the park as rapidly as the guards permit, and after all only a small proportion of those who applied was admitted. Nevertheless the grounds in the neighborhood of the fire was thronged with people. But they were people of tho better class. Their behavior was perfect. There was no noise, no tumult, no disorder, no disturbance of property, everything was quiet and solemn and decorous. Every person's judgment to be that the destruction of the buildings by fire was the best possible solution of the question of What be done with them. Long before the climax was reached thousands of people had walked back home. At the very moment Manufactures Building had caught thousands of people, without the least excitement, were leaving the grounds for home.*" That sounds like a very odd way to present what was the destruction of one of the great set of structures in

---

[51]Quote from the site Chicagology

the world. But they present more, *"Wasn't grand? What a glorious sight! A magnificent spectacle! A noble end! were the benedictions pronounced by the people as they left the grounds."* Really. Is that what the public who had to see their beautiful fair grounds burned to the ground were saying, or what the media in control of history wanted to present that people thought? I would really like to have been there that January and asked people what they really thought of that fire.

After the July fire, the destruction is far more rampant

But it is this second fire that interests me, for no one else but Bancroft seems to mention it. *"But that which was threatened on this winter night occurred a few months later. On the evening of the 5th of July some lads at play near the terminal station observed the gleam of fire within, and entering the depot tried for several minutes to stamp it out; but these few minutes were fatal to the existence of several among the most sightly temples of the Fair. It was a hot summer day; the buildings were dry as tinder; water was scarce; the fire engines far away, and a fierce gale was blowing from the southwest, fanning into a conflagration that which when first discovered was but an insignificant blaze."* This fire was supposed to have burned the Administration Buildings, the Mining, and Electricity buildings, *"both of which were quickly ablaze. To these were added, a few minutes later, the halls of Manufactures and Transportation, though through the efforts of the firemen a portion of the latter was saved. Meanwhile from the railroad terminus the conflagration had spread to the Machinery and Agricultural buildings, the one being utterly destroyed and the other damaged almost beyond recognition."*

"The burning of the Manufactures building was a sight that will never be forgotten by those who witnessed this tragic climax in the destruction of the white city. Almost as soon as the fire laid hold of it the vast semi-circular roof fell in, with its 11 acres of skylights and its 65

carloads of glass. Then it was seen that the whole interior was aflame, while from hundreds of windows tongues and jets of fire cast far on the dun waters of lake and lagoon their red and fearsome glare. Presently the frame began to totter; one after another the huge facades fell inward with a deafening roar, and of this mammoth temple of the Exposition there was nothing left, save for the lurid skeleton of a wall...As to the origin of either conflagration nothing definite was ascertained, though both were believed to be the work of incendiaries, probably of the vagrant horde which infested the streets by day and slept at night wherever darkness overtook them."

Thus the original quote labeled for people coming out to watch the Manufactures Building burn in January is likely incorrect. That must have been the July fire. I can not imagine to many coming out in January in Chicago to see much of anything. Secondly is that it in this July fire that Bancroft seems to suggest all of the large buildings were destroyed. Third is the date of July 5, one day after July 4- and I wonder if this was meant to be some sort of "fireworks" show. Again that no presentation is made of how the fires started, simply a presentation of "vagrants." It is not co-incidental that the January fire began just as public opinion seemed to be rising to find ways to keep the structures. But following the fires what remained of the fair after the fires were dismantled and deposited into landfills. The Columbia Exhibition was now only alive in photographs. Well the Statue at least seems to have remained on site, that is until 1896 when yes another fire breaks out, this time burning the statue. Or just as likely, it was removed to the hidden interior of some rich person's home as a souvenir (as we will see happened to the glass dome of the Hall of Music where President McKinley was shot in Buffalo) and then a fire blamed for its "disappearance." From what I have learned of these fairs, I think the original Statue of the Republic is still somewhere, and might be found to be made of solid gold, not gilded bronze as expected.

Wikipedia has this to say of the area after the fair/fires and its complete demolition, *"Jackson Park was returned to its status as a public park, in much better shape than its original swampy form. The lagoon was reshaped to give it a more natural appearance, except for the straight-line northern end where it still laps up against the steps on the south side of the Palace of Fine Arts/Museum of Science & Industry building. The Midway Plaisance, a park-like boulevard which extends west from Jackson Park, once formed the southern boundary of the*

University of Chicago, which was being built as the fair was closing (the university has since developed south of the Midway)."

Of the goods and exhibits not sold, many were simply kept in the US (being claimed to be too costly to ship them back to where they originated). There became a great discussion of what to do with them all. Many museums in the US were demanding them. Chicago's governing board wanted them all to stay in Chicago in one collection. So they decided to create a new Columbian Field Museum, which would house everything that had been at the fair, from history to science.[52] However there comes a very strange paragraph next in Bancroft. He writes, *"To erect a special building for the accommodation of the museum collections was not possible within the limit of time; nor was such a building required; for among the temples of the Fair, soon to be demolished and their contents removed, there was one at least that would answer the purpose for many a year to come. This was the palace of Fine Arts, the architectural gem of the Exposition and also one of its most substantial edifices, with spacious transept, nave, and galleries, affording with its annexes sufficient space for a museum almost as large as the one at the national capital. Here were arranged the various groups, including contributions from nearly all the main departments, from state and foreign exhibits, and from the Midway plaisance."* That is how the artifacts from the fair wound up in the Palace of Fine Arts originally. The problem is the above comment that claimed of there not being "enough time" to erect a building. What? They had supposedly just built the greatest set of buildings ever in world history, in a record amount of time, with 100,000 workers who should now be perfectly skilled in such building. But the claim of no time to build is telling. It makes one question everything about the fair, who built it, and why. And why say there is no time to build a museum building, at the same moment one is building a university, a cultural center, a library, large domed skyscraper and more? It all just makes no sense.

As Bancroft concluded in his book "The Columbian Exposition has fulfilled its purpose; its mission is ended; its exhibits scattered to the four quarters of the earth, and its buildings vanished into air." The question of course is just what was its real purpose, its real mission? Recall that just a few years earlier 1891, an obscure priest in a mountain village of Southern France (Berengere Sauniere of Rennes Le Chateau, the site of mystery) added an odd inscription to a pillar in his strange renovated church. It had the year 1891 and the word mission upside

---

[52]Some exhibits also found their way to the Smithsonian and to the Philadelphia Commercial Museum

down. Thus 1891 and 1681 are implied in the inversion. Perhaps an inversion is implied in this fair as well. If you turn the date 1893 over you will have E681. That could be a reference to our 681 AD or 1681 AD. I would be very curious to see if that date has an importance in the real history of Chicago.

But there is more insanity. Just ten years after the Columbian Exposition was torn down-fire bombed...Chicago built, you guesed it- a giant amusement park. A park they called "The White City" and began in 1905. It included of course "Beau Art style" buildings, a basin and a giant electric tower. They thus made the Exposition in miniature. Why? Of course most of the amusement park was for "whites only." The park when bankrupt in the depression, and only the roller rink stayed open (which became interestingly a part of the early civil rights movement in the 1940's as large demonstrations occurred in order to allow blacks to join whites in the rink). Ah the Expo lives on, in more ways than one!

So why did I spend so much detail on this Fair. Well as you can see partially it was due to the size of the event. So many buildings, so many items, so many people. To really question if in fact all of these buildings could have been built in two years as suggested, and to keep that in mind as we continue to look at the US fairs that followed after Chicago: specifically Omaha, Buffalo, St Louis and San Francisco. Each of these has similar massive buildings, more strange construction photos, odd events happening within the fairs, all with cities overcoming great fires (or in the case of San Francisco a very bizarre earthquake that almost seems to have been populated by actors as opposed to citizens). Lastly the book will conclude with a look at Ancient Rome, and what and where specifically these expositions were trying to emulate, along with a bit of a glossary of terms.

I have presented the scale here at Chicago so as to not have to again and again with each other fair. Instead I can present a few pieces of information about them that shows their similarity- in both size and concept, and present a few unique details that make the next expositions stand out. Again the complete detail of these expos are available in numerous books for free on the Internet, what this investigation is doing is trying to take those sources and find what in them can help to come to an answer one way or another on the standard history of the time.

Calendar from Tennessee Exhibition, with its Parthenon front and center.

NASHVILLE 1897

While not specifically a Worlds Fair, Tennessee held a six-month celebration to mark the one-hundredth anniversary of statehood. The Tennessee Centennial Exposition was held in Nashville from May 1 until October 30, 1897, although the state's actual centennial occurred in 1896. This seems to happen a lot, hold an anniversary the year after the anniversary should be. The Nashville fair is unique for building an actual size replica of the Parthenon in Athens, as well as having a fairly large pyramid. At least the claim is that they built them. Nashville had been given the nickname "Athens of the South." I have found no specific information to fully explain why it had this nickname. One suggestion for how the city got it its Athens title was because it was the first American city to have a public school system. A bit of a cop out explanation.

Nashville had been a place of the famous Mississippian Indian tribes, they of the mound building culture. Many mounds were supposed to have existed here, destroyed in order to build the city. Becoming the state capital in the 1840's they began to build such things as the State Capital Building (still in use) looking like a Greek ionic temple. It was supposedly built by William Strickland of Philadelphia who is claimed to have started a Greek revival movement in American architecture. He is supposed to be buried within the walls of Nashville Capitol Building (that sounds more like something the mafia would do?). Then there is the Fisk University building, supposedly built in 1866 and looks like it should be on a street corner in Prague. Or how about the columned buildings of Belmont University? Also perhaps the buildings claimed to be at the exposition. This is one of the great indicators to me as to why Nashville was given the name the Athens of the South. It was! There is much evidence that the Southern USA (prior to the white influx) was covered with buildings that would fit right in with Ancient Rome and Greece.

Tennessee Exhibition, again with lakes, beautiful buildings, and Parthenon front and center, and what appears to be the remains of a star fortress in the front of the depiction.

The exposition in Nashville also had large buildings such as the Commerce Building (256 feet by 591 feet) and the Agriculture Building (200 feet by 525 feet). The Children's Building also housed a model kindergarten, which met throughout the fair season and allowed fairgoers to see this relatively novel form of education. The Negro Building told "the story of achievement under obstacles often seemingly impossible to overcome." Interestingly it had two 90-foot twin-towers.

98

The History Building was modeled on the Erechtheon, another ancient Athenian building. Memphis (yes the city that has the name of the Egyptian Old Kingdom capital) built a pyramid as its exhibit.

Nashville Parthenon Today

But it was the Parthenon reproduction, also known as The Fine Arts building, that got most of the attention. It was "designed" by Confederate veteran William Crawford Smith. It is claimed that this building, like all the others at the fair, were built of temporary materials but...and this is the direct quote on the Wikipedia page (and seems to come from Wilbur Chrighton's book *The Parthenon in Nashville)*, "the Parthenon was not intended to be permanent, but the cost of demolishing the structure combined with its popularity with residents and visitors alike resulted in it being left standing after the Exposition." So let us get this straight. The story being presented is that ALL of the buildings were temporary, including this Parthenon. However to tear down the Parthenon was going to be too costly, so they left it standing and refurbished it in 1920 with more long lasting materials (ie stone). But what about the cost to tear down the Commerce Building or the Agricultural Building? Or all the others? They should have cost even more to tear down. But the one that looks like the Parthenon is too costly to tear down. That is as big a lie as one can present, and the reason I have for writing this book. I am not giving an answer if it was or was not built in 1897- what I am saying is that we need to do a much more thorough examination of things such as this. Another building, called the Knights of Pythias Pavilion was moved to Franklin Tennessee. It is still standing. Why were only these two buildings too costly to tear down. Can we come close to finding what is true?

99

*

OMAHA- 1898

The Trans-Mississippi Exposition was in Omaha's Kountze Park in 1898 on the 180 acre site again with lagoons, gondolas, and 21 massive buildings for a place that also called itself a "White City". Over 2.6 million people attended. The first question is where did the all come from? Omaha was a very small city in 1898, and the American West had just been opened up. That is a lot of people at the time.

The origin story of this fair claims that in 1895 Omaha banker Gordon Wattles wanted to have a World Fair in Omaha. William Jennings Bryan was a key factor in getting the fair in Omaha. He of course was the one who later was the main attorney on the side of "Bible" in the Scopes Monkey Trial in 1926. It apparently took two years just to locate a site, which meant they had but one year to build the entire fair. It purpose was to show off the "development of the American West" and though not specifically stated, to show the inferiority of the Native Indian and their "primitive" way of life. The native Indian villages were called "a living display" by the expo organizers. A modern documentary on the fair claimed it was to "showcase that the United States could take the lead in civilizing the world."

Two construction photos of Omaha Exposition

There are many photographs of the construction of the fair buildings.[53] Many are similar to the photo on the left- what does look like the creation of a temporary structure being put up of wood interior. But then there are many like those of the right, which show a completed lower building and a dome or tower being built. It is hard to tell what may have been temporary or original. That may be the point with all of these fairs. You might have had four or five originals, and by the time you throw up fifty other temporary buildings alongside them that all get painted with the same overlay, it would be almost impossible to tell one from the other.

---

[53] http://trans mississippi.unl.edu/photographs/bluff_tract.html

Government Building, Omaha 1898

Grand Court of Omaha Expo.

The main area was called The Grand Court, surrounded by magnificent Greco-Roman buildings with towers and domes. Domes, towers and columns again showcase along the white-washed painted buildings.

Yet this expo is remembered mostly for its Indian Congress, which ran from August 4 to October 31. Beyond just having a "zoo" to display natives, there the fair organizers originally wanted to have the largest gathering of Indian tribes since the whites first arrived. The idea was that the 500 members of 35 different tribes (including the Apache chief Geronimo, who was being held prisoner at Fort Sill) were to have open lectures and discussions that could be attended by the whites. This was to present the daily life, beliefs, and history of as many tribes as possible. Congress gave over $100,000 to have it, and was managed by ethnologist James Mooney. Thousands of portraits of the natives were taken, with many of the most famous coming from here. However when you look at the original collection, most native portraits were two views, one face on, the other side profile (thus look like modern mug shots) and can be seen in the link in the footnote.[54]

However once the exposition began, it was clear to the organizers that the white fairgoers were not interested in hearing what the Indians might have to say, and instead just wanted to see dances, games, and ceremonials. Soon promoters were influenced by The Improved Order of Redmen (a white fraternal organization) who called to have the congress stopped completely and instead show off battles between whites and Indians, where the whites would always win. It underscored the message that the natives were a race on their way to extinction and thus needed to submit to white rule. A 5,000 seat grandstand was soon erected to have these fake battles. The other main activity demanded by the whites were re-enactments and the Ghost Dance, which caused many concerns in the government given that the US Army murdered hundreds of Ghost Dancers in 1890 at Wounded Knee. Thus the idea of an actual Congress where various Indians shared their views with whites was long dead, and instead they started what became the standard Western movie themes of the 1950's. Indians and their connection with nature was quickly seen as something whites should not focus on.

One US senator claimed at the fair, "miracaulous is the growth of the Mississippi region...it will support a population of 25 million without taxing its resources to oblivion...Science will discover new applications for overcoming the obstacles of nature. The inventions of Edison will replenish the treasuries of the world with the gold of its mountain ranges, and the discoveries of Tesla may convert the wasted winds and rivers into applied energy that will carry on all operations of industry without the intervention of human labour."[55] Yes the wind and rivers are nothing but waste, and all nature but an obstacle. This is how people

---

54

they can be found at
http://trans-mississippi.unl.edu/photographs/.html?&fq=collection:
%22American%20Indians%201898%20photo%20album%22
[55]Rydell p135

103

thought then, and sadly still thought now. As this book is showing, there was a time that no one thought like this, and may have in fact lived in great harmony with this place.

There is an oddity I want to point out about the photographs of the fair. Most of them have original copyright dates directly on the photos. Generally of course they list 1898, the year of the fair. A few appear with the year 1897. However, there are photos with dates of years such as 1892, even 1858. The photo of the US Government Building above is one of the ones with an 1892 copyright date, one of the reasons I included it in this book. Why is there an 1892 copyright on the photo of the Government Building? I don't think that is some sort of casual mistake. They took this copyright stuff seriously even then. Could we really be seeing buildings photographed eight years prior to the fair? So we really have to ask, just what year was this fair photographed.

Still it is interesting to read the historians discuss the speedy way the fair supposedly came up and didn't last. These are typical quotes, "But it was intentionally built cheap and temporary—this was the only way Omaha could afford such a spectacular place! To show the cheapness of the buildings at the expo, check this out: In November 1898, the Nebraska Building was sold for $470 to a new company. That amount in 2015 dollars? $12,819.99. These weren't well-built structures, and people then knew it, even if people today don't quite understand or accept that."[56] Ok that is the standard historical explanation for these fairs. As you know so far I just don't believe that story, but this is what you will come up with again and again, as if no historian is actually willing to just take ten minutes and think about what they are presenting from the standpoint of the actual architecture and building construction required.

When the fair ended they only demolished a few buildings, and decided to have another smaller fair the following year. After this second fair, a railroad car packed with demolition equipment arrived on November 4th 1899. It took only until January 1900 to have basically demolished the entire thing. What wasn't demolished was, you guessed it, destroyed in a mysterious fire just a few months later (June 1900). After that there was again nothing left.

---

[56] http://trans-mississippi.unl.edu/

*
BUFFALO 1901

Buffalo's Pan-American Exposition. Who built these?

Buffalo had a Worlds Fair in 1901. Yes Buffalo. Ok Buffalo did have the 8th largest population in the US at the time, and did have a proximity to both the tourist attraction of Niagara Falls, and closeness to New York City. But still it is hard to place Buffalo in the same breath as Paris, London, Barcelona, Chicago and other Worlds Fair hosts. Why is the city even named Buffalo? The origin for the name is in fact unknown. The standard claim is that it is named after nearby Buffalo Creek. Ok, but then how did the creek get its name. There were no Buffalo around this area when the white Europeans supposedly arrived. One claim suggests it comes from French fur traders calling the river the Beau Fleive (Beautiful River) but I think that is a stretch. Some claim the creek was named long ago by Indians when Buffalo were this far east. Other suggestions are equally odd. So in fact no one has any idea why the city has the name Buffalo. All of its growth as a city is claimed to come from the building of the Erie Canal in 1825. Buffalo, like Chicago, has a number of old structures in the city- churches and government buildings, hotels and the like. Again it really makes you wonder where they came from, and who built them in such a short period of time.

Their Pan American Exposition was held in 1901, that also began on that May 1 date. It occupied a massive 350 acres, and again was supposedly built of temporary structures, of which only a few survived (such as the current Buffalo History Museum). Several guidebooks were published for the fair, including Rand McNally. Anyone going there said they were going to "do the pan." Many of the guides suggest the reader take a day or two and visit Toronto, Hamilton and Niagara Falls Canada. Thomas Edison shot much video at this fair (though it is grainy) which is interesting as again the electricity of the fair was won again by Nikola Tesla and Westinghouse.

It was at this fair that US President William McKinley was assassinated in the Temple of Music. His last speech before he was shot discussed that, "*Expositions are the timekeepers of progress. They record the world's advancement. They stimulate the energy, enterprise, and intellect of the people; and quicken human genius. They go into the home. They broaden and brighten the daily life of the people. They open mighty storehouses of information to the student.*" McKinley at the time was very popular. The US had just won the Spanish-American War and gained several territorial acquisitions from it. This fair was supposed to in some way glorify the new expansionist flavour the US had taken up. Pan Americanism was the idea that the US was to be in control of all of the Americas North and South. And this was reflected in the logo for the fair.

Logo of the Pan-American Exposition

The logo had North and South America symbolized by two women whose dresses form the shapes of the continents, while their hands joined over Central America. It was painted by Raphael Beck, who used two specially selected beauty contest winners (Maxine Elliot and Maude Coleman Woods) to model for it. Oddly there may have been a second message in the logo besides the union of north and south America, for Elliot came from Maine (key union state in the Civil War) while Coleman Woods (called the most beautiful woman in Virginia by the Daughters of the Confederacy) was from a key Southern State.

Buffalo construction?

But when it comes to construction photos, this is the hardest fair to find them of. The Buffalo History Museum has a few, but they are very dubious. The one above is just one guy standing inside of one of the peristyle courts with no construction at all happening.

Construction of Electric Tower 1900

Above is the giant electrical tower. Looks pretty complete to me. So far no one has shown how the great tower, some 390 feet high, could be built out of some two by fours and plaster. The photos of its demolition has the thing crashing into the ground like a falling jumbo jet. It looks as solid as can be on its landing, not something made out of wood and lime-hemp.

Construction in Buffalo 1901

This is supposed to be a photo of workers. They do look like laborers for sure, but they are all wearing painting smocks (so not building but painting) and the guys in front are obviously making it "look like they are working." My guess is what we are seeing a lot of at these fairs is the use of plaster, but plastering over already existing brick buildings. That would not only hide the original brick work, but make it then impossible to differentiate between a similar plastered over small wood structure that had been built beside it. Another theory, and one we will put to the test next in St Louis, is that much of the fair was there at the site- just not above ground. It was from such an old time, that it had been covered with mud in the 100 years previous from what are called the "mudfloods." Thus the work of the fair workers was not to construct the sites, but to dig them out, repair as needed, plaster overtop, finally paint them. Voila, 350 acres of buildings go up on a few years.

While Chicago was called the "White City," and Omaha the "New White City," the buildings in Buffalo featured much color and as such it was named "The Rainbow City." Some 2000 sculptures (some new and some historical) could be found on every part of the fair site. Huge buildings are again here such as the "Manufactures," "Liberal Arts," "Machines," "Transportation," "Agriculture," and "Electricity." "Most of the buildings at the exposition were designed in what was referred to as "Spanish Renaissance Style."

The Federal Government Building occupied the entire eastern Esplanade of the Exposition and was 130 feet by 418 feet, connected by colonnades to two annexes for Fishery and Agriculture, each 100 square feet. The total exhibition space was 75,000 square feet. The central dome was 250 high and topped by a 20-foot statue of 'victory'. The Temple of Music was the only one of the "temporary buildings" whose interior was finished. It was 150 feet on each side, the center dome rising to 180 feet outside, 53 feet 9 inches from the floor inside. The four major pieces of sculpture were on each corner of the building were intended to symbolize the major categories of Music. Inside were 4PM concerts with the largest organ in the US, while at night seating for concerts was 2,200. The Women's Building was one the site previously as was used by the Country Club of Buffalo for golf and polo grounds. The New York State Building, called the only building planned to be permanent (only because it happens to still be there) is now the Buffalo History Museum. The south side looks like the Parthenon in Athens. Above the columns are fine detailed sculpture.

Buffalo Electrical Tower in 1901

In the center of the fair was the 395 foot high Electrical Tower. On top of the tower was a golden statue called The Goddess of Light (mirroring the golden statue in Chicago). One of the real oddities for me of this fair in the photographs is to see just how much electricity is being generated. All of the buildings are lit up like Christmas trees. Where is all the energy coming from? The history claims it comes again from Nikola Tesla. Walter Hines Page claimed at the time, "The Tower is a great center of brilliancy. There are perhaps not a half million electric bulbs, but there are hundreds and thousands of them and you are willing to believe that there may be millions. It shines like diamonds, a transparent, soft structure of sunlight." Supposedly special turbines were set up at Niagara Falls, to bring power to the Electrical building at the fairgrounds.

I would speculate the giant Electrical Tower and the Electrical Building (loaded with domes) in front of the lagoon (somehow connecting them with the energy of water), are likely the manufacture of the energy for the lights. What is more odd when it comes to all the electricity on display, is that very few of the interiors of key buildings (such as the Exposition hospital's operating room where the President was taken) had any lights.

But for all the nice Roman buildings, and pleasant lagoons- this was a very screwed up fair. First is The Johnstown Flood Midway concession, which was a very "graphic" presentation of the 1889 disaster in Johnstown, Pennsylvania caused by a dam breaking and resulting in the loss of 2,200 lives. It cost 25 cents and ran every thirty minutes. An exhibit to show off a massive amount of deaths from a flood, and the May 4, 1901 edition of the Buffalo Times called it "wonderful."[57] Why do I think this is important? Because I think this is really a depiction·of what Alternate Historians refer to as the mudflood. A world wide event, though not necessarily at the same moment of time (perhaps triggered by some sort of sound or energy weapon locally) that produced Biblical floods, and left cities covered in many feet of mud. Whether Johnstown itself had a dam burst, or whether that was just a story to explain the obvious flood damage from "the event," I get the sense that this Johnstown exhibit was really there to symbolically reflect the worldwide destruction over the last 100 or so years (which will be further mentioned in the final chapter). It was ok if these Expositions lost money, for they had a deeper purpose all together, and I feel that was a sort of historical brainwashing.

Stadium, aka Coliseum, looking past a tower of the Electrical Building, 1901

[57]Buffalo Tribune May 4, 1901

Native Indians were brought in again to have giant battle re-enactments with US cavalry troops in a 12,000 seat stadium that was "an imitation of the Coliseum in Rome." "*Built as a temporary structure, the enormous stadium became a topic of speculation as the Exposition's closing neared. A few wanted to maintain it as a permanent addition to the North Buffalo area. But it was owned by the Exposition company and stood on leased land, and so there was no serious contemplation of preserving an all-wooden structure whose decorative features were covered with staff. Like the rest of the Exposition buildings, it only appeared substantial. A news item from March 25, 1902, said, 'The great Stadium of the Exposition has been attacked by the wreckers and it will be laid low in a few days'.*" [58] Further photos of this stadium show a great amount of what can only be called "weathering" including what appears to be a type of mold growing on some of the walls. It seems like an awful lot of mold for a structure only supposed to be one year old.

Basically the battles were set up to be like a giant 1950's movie Western, Edison has some of it filmed, and when watching it it seems to be lines of two sides firing shots at each other, but at no time does anyone pretend to die or be hurt. The Indians were there as part of the showing off the "defeated nations" just destroyed by the US army. Tepees and exhibits were set up to show their "primitive tools" and "primitive life" to further present the great military power of the US to defeat them, and the great consumer goods that the eastern white people had that made them superior to the natives. Margaret Creighton wrote in her book, "The most shocking event in the fair was the public slaughter of 700 dogs, many taken from animal shelters or snatched off streets. It was held over two days in front of 20,000 spectators. The Indian Congress, made up of several tribes, carried out the executions with Geronimo, on loan from an Oklahoma prison, killing the first dog with a bow and arrow. The dogs were then eaten."[59]

But the racism did not stop there. A popular part of the Midway was "The Old Plantation." The Buffalo Evening News described (and I quote the article exactly) "*Genuine southern darkies, two hundred of them, ranging in years from wee, toddling pickininies to negroes, grey and bent with age, can be seen each day at the Exposition at their*

---

[58]Panam1901.org Other events were also held at the Stadium inclding baseball and football games, cattle shows and parades

[59]*The Rise and Fall of the Rainbow City*, by Margaret Creighton- found in Buffalo News article review of her book.

different occupations and pastimes. Lovers of negro melodies will have a feast. Many of the darkies will be selected because of their special talents as singers and banjo players and they will dance and sing to the seductive tinkling of instruments exactly as the Negroes of the South used to do in the long, long ago."[60] The Buffalo Express suggested, "If you like to hear coon songs and dances and banjo music, go to the Old Plantation and spend a very pleasant hour or so."[61] You can find several photos of it on the net if you good search "cakewalk and old plantation." Expositions and racism seem to be tied together during this period.

*

President McKinley arriving at the Temple of Music, shortly before being assassinated.

The Buffalo Exposition is most known for the shooting of President McKinley, twice in the stomach by Leon Czolgosz in the Temple of Music on September 6. What was shocking about the aftermath was the hospital and operating area at the fair had no interior lighting (though outside was 10,000 electric lights). They had to hold up a mirror to reflect in the rays of the sun for a local doctor, not trained in such surgeries, to do the operation. A nationwide hunt went out looking for any "anarchist" that might have been a friend of Czolgosz. Anyone he had even spoken to for the past few weeks was arrested and held for questioning for weeks. Meanwhile the news on the president was that his health was continuously improving, until September 12 when it was reported he was getting worse and then died on the 13th.

[60] *High Hopes, The Rise and Decline of Buffalo* by Mark Goldman

[61] *Mckinley, Murder and the Pan American Exposition,* by Roger Peckinpaugh

The trial of Czolgosz started on September 23 (just ten days after the death of the President), and lasted only 2 days. His two appointed attorneys basically argued nothing. They did not speak to the client and called no witnesses or entered testimony. He was quickly convicted and died in the electric chair on October 29, 1901. He was quickly buried and had acid poured over his body. There can be almost no doubt that this assassination was similar to the Kennedy assassination, and inside job that was quickly covered up so that the choice of leader- here Theodore Roosevelt, could be in charge. The electric chair actually turned out to be a big part of the fair and is connected to the rivalry between Tesla and Edison. Edison had previously tried to show Tesla's alternating current was dangerous, and had staged public electrocutions of animals - including dogs and a horse - using Tesla's technology. Edison was the first to use the electric chair on a prisoner, William Kemmler at the Auburn, New York prison in 1890. Then 11 years later, Edison was back at the same prison, helping with Czolgosz execution. "Edison went so far as to a create a filmed re-enactment of the execution, so he could brand anything associated with electricity with his own name."[62]

There was another execution. The Midway also had animals presented by Frank C. Bostock, "the animal king, a man of unbounded courage and resources, before whom all animals cower." Sounds like a lovely man...but it gets worse. Bostock had recently acquired Jumbo, a nine-ton elephant from the British Army, where it had been decorated by Queen Victoria for bravery in the Afghanistan Wars. So how does he treat the elephant? Bostock claimed that by the end of the fair Jumbo had stopped eating, and even tried to attack him. So he decided to have the elephant killed, and with a public execution at the fair grounds with tickets costing fifty cents. He said: "It is likely that Jumbo will be hanged, or choked to death with chains, in which case other elephants will be used."

Opposition to the plan was immediate from the Buffalo mayor and fair organizers. The problem they had was not with killing the elephant, but the method being used on the fair grounds, they would only allow it to go on if the elephant was electrocuted. Yes electrocuted. Sunday November 3, 7000 people came to witness it. The elephant was set up to long electrical wires, Bostock gave a speech of Jumbo's military service, and how his time in the midway caused him to become

[62] *Stuff of Genius:Tongues of Living Flame: Nikola Tesla and the Pan American Exposition of 1901* by Christian Sager Nov 1, 2013

a killer. Then the switch was pulled and and electricity shot through the elephant. But Jumbo did not die. "The crowd, almost spontaneously, started to laugh and Bostock, himself incredulous, promised over the din of the laughter that he would refund the tickets. Only later did he realize that Jumbo's hide had the effect of rubber and was impossible to penetrate. Jumbo's execution was stayed."[63] These are the people who shaped our modern world, and this Buffalo fair is a great example of how it is run- slave exhibits, dog killings, electrocuting prized elephants, co-ordinating presidential assassinations.

With the McKinley's assassination the excitement for the fair all but died with him. November 1, the day of closing, was called Buffalo Day with the hopes of drawing one last large crowd. What happened by the evening was a riot, "People went mad. They were seized with the desire to destroy. Depredation and destruction were carried on in the boldest manner all along the Midway. Electric light bulbs were jerked from their posts and thousands of them were smashed on the ground. Some of the Midway restaurants were crushed into fragments under the pressure of the mob as if they were so much pasteboard. Windows were shattered and doors were kicked down. Policemen were pushed aside as if they were stuffed ornaments. The National Glass Exhibit was completely destroyed. Pabst's Cafe was demolished and Cleopatra's needle was torn to the ground."[64]

By 1902 the fair began to be destroyed, by Harris Wrecking Company of Chicago. A local committee was formed to buy and preserve the Electric Tower as a lasting monument to the exposition, but failed to raise the necessary funds. On January 20, 1902, the statue of the Goddess of Light was sold to the Humphrey Popcorn Company of Cleveland, and the tower was finally torn down. The fair was gone.[65]

I happened to be watching some youtube clips of some people who film themselves exploring abandoned buildings. One they were in was an old TB hospital/asylum near Buffalo. The hospital, built in 1909, has a giant domed rotunda. Ok that's strange. A comment on the video had me look into it, and yes there is a connection to the fair. The hospital- JN Adam Memorial Hospital in Pennysburg NY, was built between 1909-1912. It is huge. Unfortunately I could not find one photo

---

[63]Goldman, High Hopes

[64]Goldman, High Hopes

[65]Of course Buffalo built a new Electrical Tower in downtown in 1912, that definitely while nice, comes no where close to the grandeur and seemed special nesss of the one at the Exposition.

that can be described as Public Domain, so you are going to have to do the google search yourself to see it. What is remarkable is that the beautiful glass on top of the dome is the very same piece of glass that was at the top of The Temple Of Music at the Buffalo Fair. Yes the place where the president was assassinated. It is listed as having been donated as a gift to the hospital by Buffalo mayor Adam. Huh? So the mayor kept the glass where the president was assassinated, obviously as some sort of trophy. I am sure the group that had Kennedy killed has a number of souvenirs. So this hospital was started with the souvenir of the assassination. I just wanted to mention that when you look into fairs, parts of them show up in the strangest places.

A week after the fair was the report that it had lost over $6 million and that the Company would have to default on over $3.5 million in bonds. But Milburn claimed that the money spent was not foolish but that the Pan American was "a masterpiece," and the city its "chosen showcase." Yet Milburn did not stay in Buffalo, but left for New York and a partnership in a law firm. Yes the Buffalo fair was a money loser, had a president assassinated, racism presented in the most foul ways, animals murdered. You would think that might be enough to stop the whole business of Expositions finally. But no, they decided that the next one needs to be even bigger!

ST. LOUIS 1904

Festival Hall, Cascades and Lagoon, 1904

The next US World Fair was three years later in St. Louis, named The Louisiana Purchase Exposition (to honor the 1803 purchase of what is now much of Central USA from Napoleonic France). They also demanded, and got, the Summer Olympic games of that year to co-incide with the fair. The Jackson Park fair was actually bigger than the one in Chicago, and not just by a small amount, it dwarfed Chicago's. The fair inspired the song "Meet Me in St. Louis, Louis", which became central in the 1944 movie of the same name starring Judy Garland. A few books I recommend for this fair to see photos of it are *The Forrest City 1904*, by William Rau official photographer, *Louisiana and the Fair: an exposition of the world* by JW Buel (a nine volume, 4000 page treatise), *Final Report of the Louisiana Purchase Exposition Commission,* and the German book *Ansichen von der Weltausstelling* (a English book partially translated to German. All four books can be referenced via studylove.org 1904 page for St. Louis.

*

This was the area of the famous Mississippi mound builders, and one of their cities, Cahokia, is still in east St Louis. With pyramids, temples and a structure called "Woodhenge" it is one of Native Americas great early sites. French explorers were not supposed to begin coming to the area until 1700's. The census of 1772 claims the village to be 637 people. The Louisiana Purchase happens in 1803, and right after the army team of Cpt Meriweather Lewis and Lt William Clark go on a two year odyssey across the entire of Indian Territory from Pittsburgh to the Pacific coast. They were to explore and map the country, study the plant animal life, and create trade routes with the local native Indians. Of course the real mission of their journey might have been much different. To find out what other great deserted cities in the newly taken land might be. They too would be the historical focus of an Exposition, that in Portland 1905.

The old St. Louis County courthouse in downtown St. Louis, Missouri, commonly known as the Old Courthouse. How much court activity are they expecting in the 1820's when it was supposedly built?

St. Louis began to grow. In 1816 work was started on the above courthouse. Here a city with less than 2,000 of population, in the middle of the continent with basically no roads, can just throw that building up in a few years. Where did all the stone come from, and how was it all transported on horse back and wagons? Just how many people were going to court every day that this was needed?

The 1840's are claimed to to be a time of great immigration from Irish and Germans, as well as a huge influx of black slaves. It became a city of jazz and blues music, as well as a key chapter in early pro baseball. 1849 seems to be a bad year. First a cholera epidemic is said to kill 5,000 people. Then a huge fire breaks out (what city with ancient buildings does not have a fire?) supposedly started by accident on a steam boat. More likely 1849 is marked out as the year they began to bring in new people to this found or captured city. History prior to 1849 is basically made up, and what we can even remotely call history began in this year.

Laying bricks on city streets, 1900

The above photo is claimed to be from 1900, and it shows the laying down of brick streets over what had obviously been just dirt mud roads. So all of St Louis's fabulous architecture was built for 100 years but they never thought to make a street in order to make the transport of materials easier. They built things like the courthouse above, but laying down a proper street first was just not something worth their time.

*

119

Work in 1902 with horses pulling out tree stumps. Glad they only needed ten guys and five horses to help get this site ready in two years time.

Forest Park, in southern St. Louis had been created in 1876 (that ceremonial date again). By 1890 three million people per year were visiting the park thanks to newly built Subway Lines that ran there. It this spot that was chosen for the exposition as according to the site atthefair because, "The park was at a central point between the north and south of town, in place as well as good water pressure. Furthermore, stately private streets such as Westmoreland Place and Portland Place were located near the park." Many of the giant homes of the period are still there. So my first question is, why would the rich elite- who really enjoy their privacy and isolation from the commoners, want to be besieged by millions of people, not just for the fair but for the years of its building? These are the same people who would be putting in the money to have it, so they could easily have demanded any other site. But it is presented as if the fair close to these rich homes is a good idea. Again that makes no sense. It is more likely that the site was chosen because of what was already there (either above ground or buried in mud). The "mansion homes" were just a part of the original city and were in that location because of it. The elite homes were stuck with the fair for a few years in order to deal with the ancient buildings there that had to be "dealt with."

Back to standard history. Before construction could begin, an environmental group started a lawsuit to stop the cutting down the large woodland area in the northwest. A compromise was reached and the committee said they would only use 657 acres of the park and leave the rest. New property directly west was leased, that would become Washington University. Why exactly Missouri would name its main university for Washington is unclear. Of curse, with no surprise, the University chose giant Gothic style architecture for its buildings.

The first architect meeting occurred on June 27, 1901. The Designer of Works for the fair was Isaac Taylor. Taylor has a similar history to Burnham in Chicago, having designed 215 large buildings, mainly in St Louis. Exactly how he gained the skills to be the foremost architect of the Midwest is up for debate, as he graduated university in 1868 with a degree in Classical Languages but was claimed to be an expert in Gothic architecture somehow. He was then picked up for work by JI Barnetts firm shortly after graduation (a similar story to Burnham's rise). The main adviser for the park layout was George Kessler. Born in Germany he moved to the US early in life. While famous New York landscaper Olmstead (who designed the Chicago Exhibition) did not hire him, he did suggest that Kessler "educate himself about nature through reading, reflection, and excursions, and to aim to free himself from German associations in order to expand his capabilities and to not limit his influence and opportunities." He eventually got work in New York that then expanded worldwide. He is credited with over 200 projects for 26 communities, 26 park systems, 49 parks, 46 estates and residences, and 26 schools from Shanghai to Mexico City. Of course he too is a freemason of 32 degree, of Lodge 316 in Kansas City.[66]

---

[66]Wikipedia sources

Re routing the river to also build the lagoons and canals. Think how many shovel fulls of dirt had to be carried by horse and wagon just to excavate what is in this photo (a small part of the digging process)

Julius Pitzman, another fair adviser, presented problems with the Des Peres river to the architect group. The problem of its route, along with high chances of flood, meant it would have to be worked on before building could begin. The decision was to straighten the river, and have it moved underground. The entire river was said to have been completely re-landscaped, rerouted by the Rich Construction Company in just 65 days. A major river was re-routed and moved underground in 65 days! December 20, 1901, was the groundbreaking ceremony (which will later become quite a source of controversy). They burned wood to thaw the frozen ground, in order to pound in the oak spike, signifying the beginning of construction. Because there is no better time to start building a massive exhibition than the middle of winter. The statue of St. Louis would be placed on that spot.

St Louis Construction, image 1

St Louis Construction, image 2

123

St Louis Construction, image 3

As for the construction, of course the presentation is as strange as Chicago. There are hundreds of photos available, a good place to start is the website athefair. The photos on the previous page are a good example of what one will find. The usual is the standard mostly complete buildings that are covered with scaffolding. The claim is that one million feet of scaffolding was used in the project. But again. But again are they using the scaffolding to build, or are the using it to refurbish or paint? The second and third photos are also quite common, that is completed buildings standing alone in an area that can best be described as a mudpit. The second one has a few ladders propped up against it, I think trying to make it look like something is being done with the building. The third photos helps provide some scale to the size of this project, and think of how many shovels of earth would be needed just to landscape the area.

It was more than just the 200, some massive, buildings. Thirty miles of new streets were created, while seventy miles of roads were resurfaced. Trees were axed or replanted. Thousands of tree stumps were removed, countless cubic feet of soil had to be graded, plus the hotels, restaurants, the midway called The Pike, the Great Basin and Cascades created. Again this is all supposed to be magically done in just over two years, ALL by horse drawn equipment with no machines, electric tools and the like (though a few steam powered pieces were claimed to be used). And when you see the photos it is all very very odd.

124

When I showed these series of photos to my building contractor friend he became very clear on what he was seeing. The first thing he asked was, "Where are all the workmen? I mean to build this you need 20-30,000 guys. Where are they? All on holiday? And where is the evidence they are even there. No accessible building materials, no tools, no food areas, no evidence anyone has been here for a long time. It is like this is day one and someone is walking into to take a photo. This is very very strange."

So exciting was the building was that supposedly 100,000 visitors came each Sunday to watch the process. But then you see the construction photos, and there are usually no more than two or three workers in any photo. There does not seem to be much work going on. It seems not one of the photos was ever taken on one of the Sundays when all the visitors were there. That would have made an interesting photo, the crowds gawking at the massive project. You would think a newspaper would want a photo of that. But no, I can not find one. Just photos with no workers, one or two horse carts. What is also interesting is that in Mural Halstead's 1904 book referred to the fairgrounds as "the city of mighty magicians." Is he giving a "Bancroft type" sly reference to something?

*

Early Photoshop?

125

A few of the photos even appear to be an early form of photoshop. The one above is a good example, with an original photo of some guys constructing a wooden frame, but a piece of a statue that was used in the fair obviously "double exposed" onto the original to make it look like it was there. Any photo expert can see the double exposure quite clearly, the strange black shading around the statue in the above photo. It adds to the dubious nature of whole the construction photos.

At least this above buildings has evidence of being built in simple materials. And I think that is the catch. Some buildings were in deed thrown up in a temporary manor to make it so no one could easily tell the difference between a new and old structure. I am clear that temporary buildings were put up, they had to be (especially all the specialty structures along the Midways). Careful look of many do reveal they were built cheaply and in the time frame. And that is what makes it so hard to really understand what we are seeing with these expositions.

So again take the photo above. Was this built or dug out. What gets me most though in this photo is the utility poles. What are they? Telephone, telegraph, electricity? And of course just how old are they? There is suggestion that the old civilization had free wireless energy that used utility poles without wires to move the energy (and perhaps even a simple type of Internet-like technology) into everyone's homes. Later the same poles had wires added to them in the 1890's to hook up the "new" paid technology that we are familiar with today.

Again the fair was to open in 1903, but like Chicago had to be delayed one year to get everything built. Again I don't think so. I think it took two years to refurbish and paint the main stuff, and build all the add ons like the giant structures along the Pike. The only things left today are the St Louis Art Museum, and The Birdcage at zoo. Again why only build just one real building and fake ones for the rest? Why is there this idea at each of these fairs to build just one real structure?

*

US Government Building

The Fair was opened in 1904 by its President Francis with these remarks, "Open ye gates; spring wide ye portals; enter in, ye sons of men and behold the achievement of your race; learn the lesson here taught, and gather from it inspiration to still greater achievements."[67] I found interesting the list of it being a portal, and behold the achievements. What achievements and what race is being referred to?

The exposition is massive, twice as large as Chicago at over 1,200 acres (4,9 Km2) with over 1,500 buildings, connected by some 75 miles (121 km) of roads and walkways. Chicago was "only" 693 acres. The Palace of Agriculture alone covered some 20 acres (81,000 m2). Again we are dealing with and exposition of giant structures, domes, towers, columns, arches, lakes, canals. Two years to build from scratch 1,200 acres of buildings, roads, fountains, sewers, lagoons and all the landscaping.

There is no better place to start than the Palace of Agriculture, the Exposition's largest. The building measured 546 feet wide and 1,660 feet long, and had the height of an eight story building. A walk of three-quarters of a mile was required to simply pass around it. Inside were 10,000 exhibits of fifteen countries and forty-two states. On the east side of it's exterior was the largest rose garden in the world, covering 10 acres and displaying 1,000,000 flowers. To the north was the Floral

---

[67]Pictorial History of the Lousiana, Halstead
127

Clock which had 13,000 flowering plants covering its face. At night, it was illuminated by a over thousand lights. It was the larges clock in the world. Operated by compressed air, the minute hand was 75 feet long and weighed 2,700 pounds and moved five feet every minute. The hour hand was 50 feet long. Interestingly cameras could be used anywhere on the fairgrounds except within the Agriculture Building. That peeks my curiosity right there. So what was there inside of that building that they organizers did not want anyone to photograph?

Palace of Fine Arts

The Palace of Fine Arts was supposedly the the only permanent building. Built by Cass Gilbert- the architect who designed the United States Supreme Court building, "he often used the Beaux Arts style to reflect the optimistic American sense that the nation was the heir of Greek democracy, Roman law and Renaissance humanism. For the Palace in St Louis, Gilbert was heavily inspired by the Baths of Caracalla in Rome, Italy." Again that direct imitation of specific buildings in Ancient Rome. The structure was built from Bedford stone, the highest quality limestone in the United States. All the 11,000 art exhibits were on the ground floor, with 134 sky-lights.

Administration Building, now Brookens Hall at the University...this was claimed to be built in 1900...and can be seen in the distance of early 1902 photographs of clearing Jackson Park land.

The Mines Building was 525 by 750 feet, Transportation Building 525 by 1300, Manufactures 525 by 1200, Electricity 525 by 659 feet. The Administration Building was built for the University, and was made to look like a Tudor England castle. The Fraternity Building was 200 by 300 feet and had eighty rooms for fraternal orders. Entirely surrounded by lagoons, the Palace of Education and Social Economy, was situated facing west on the Grand Basin. Fairgoers gained entrance by walking over monumental bridges. Visitors could view an elementary school actually having their classes, or attend a college lecture.

Festival Hall and Cascades

The Festival Hall (used for concerts) was the centerpiece of the Fair. Also designed by Cass Gilbert, it was 200 feet in diameter and 200 feet high. The Festival Hall's dome at 165 feet in diameter was larger than St. Peter's Basilica in Rome. Evelyn Longman's "Victory" statue, stood on top of the dome. The building had an auditorium for 3,500 people, and the world's new largest pipe organ built by the Los Angeles Art Organ Company (which went bankrupt as a result). The massive instrument had 10,059 pipes and was capable of 17,179,869,183 distinct tonal effects, and needed 10 train cards to transport it to St Louis. Afterwards it was purchased by John Wanamaker for his new Wanamaker's store in Philadelphia where it became known as the Wanamaker Organ. The famous Bronze Eagle in the Wanamaker Store also came from the Fair. It features hundreds of hand-forged bronze feathers and was the centerpiece of one of the German exhibits. In front of the Festival Hall were the Cascades. A series of waterfalls in which pumps pushed 45,000 gallons of water a minute through man-made falls into the Grand Basin. Scott Joplin wrote the ragtime song "Cascades" in honor of them.

The Missouri State building was the largest of the state building. "Though it had sections with marble floors and heating and air conditioning, it was planned to be a temporary structure. However, it burned the night of November 18–19, just eleven days before the Fair was to end." Most of the interior was destroyed, but some contents were rescued without damage, including some furniture and much of the contents of the fair's Model Library. Since the fair was almost over, the building was not rebuilt. Of course it is interesting that the one building that claims to have real marble and even heating and air conditioning burns in a fire, a fire that destroyed ONLY this one building.

*

Many new inventions were presented here such as a "wireless telephony" unit or radiophone. Music or spoken messages were transmitted from an apparatus within the **Palace of Electricity** to a telephone receiver out in the courtyard. The receiver, which was attached to nothing, when placed to the ear allowed a visitor to hear the transmission. This radiophone, invented by Alexander Graham Bell, consisted of a transmitter which transformed sound waves into light waves and a receiver which converted the light waves back into sound waves. This technology developed into the radio and early mobile phones. Again I wonder how much the "Palace of Electricity" had with the ability of this device to work. I am sure the tower of the Palace would be working similar to a modern cell phone tower. That means they were displaying the cell phone in 1904...but could not get another one up and running (for the public anyway) until after 1990. It makes one wonder now about the supposed cell phones claimed to be seen in some 1920's silent movies...they might be actual cell phones given this St Louis information.

An early version of the fax machine was also presented, as were the X ray machine. As well early automobiles were on display and key to say here are models were powered by gasoline, steam, and electricity. Yes they were showcasing electrical cars in 1904! Just how much has been hidden from us for so long. Added to this was an airplane contest, and led to St Louis getting the nickname of "The Flight City" as well as Lindbergh naming his plane The Spirit of St. Louis. Another major exhibit was the Infant incubator – Although infant incubators were invented in the year 1888, they were not being well used so they began to display them at various Worlds Fairs. This piece of medical equipment helped the baby with compromised immune systems by providing a sanitary environment to reduce the likelihood of acquiring an infection. Each incubator was an air-tight glass box with a metal frame. Hot air was pumped into the container to keep a constant temperature. Ten nurses cared for twenty-four neo-natal babies while in the infant incubators. The exhibit required an entrance fee of twenty-five cents and visitors could also purchase souvenirs and refreshments from the adjoining shop and cafe.

*

The Pike

The Pike was the name for the fair's long midway street was more than just a few booths and carnival rides. It was almost 1.5 miles long, and doctors warned weaker patients not to go to it out of fear they would collapse from "trying to see it all."While the Chicago Ferris wheel was there and of curse basic rides and the like, take a gander at the world experience the visitor could enjoy. It so dwarfed what was at Chicago I have to present some of it to you to get a sense of some of what it was, for it was like a giant worldwide travel experience, accentuated by thousands of actors. Each exhibit had a giant restaurant seating as many as 3,000 people.

"Ancient Rome" was a colossal exhibit, with over 400 actors employed to give the visitor illusion of going back in time to a life of gladiators. A large arena, called the Hippodrome showcased chariot race, jousting, boxing, and gladiatorial clashes with 200 persons, 40 animals (including tigers, lions, and leopards). The finale was a reproduction of Nero's Rome burning (oddly this is the exact Roman period I think these expositions are mirroring discussed in chapter 7). "Tyrolean Alps" was a nine acre reproduction of the alpine region in Bavaria, Germany. It had 21 village cottages, a cathedral, and gigantic mountains of staff. Visitors could ride a simulated tram car though the Alps, where real cattle and goats would be in pasture. Dancers and musicians entertained the crowds. "Jerusalem" covered eleven acres, and included 22 streets and 300 buildings. Replicated were the stable in which Jesus Christ was said to be born, the Golden Gate, The Mosque of Omar, and the Church of Holy Sepulcher. Over 1000 people from Jerusalem traveled to the United States to participate and work at this exhibit. Like at Chicago one could walk down the "Streets of Cairo" and smoke a waterpipe, ride a camel, haggle for carpets, or walk through a replica of Luxor Temple. At the "Streets of Seville" one saw a replica of the Plaza de Toros in Madrid and Gypsy Lane of Barcelona. "The Great Siberian" was a train ride that utilized illusion to make one believe they were on the great cross-Russian railway. The "Irish Village" was entering via a replica of St. Lawrence's Gate, "Paris" replicated France during medieval times, and there was "Constantinople", "the Chinese Village", and "the Streets of Old St Louis."

Boer War Exhibit

There were more than just world trips. Frank E. Fillis produced what was supposedly "the greatest and most realistic military spectacle known in the history of the world". It was a mock battle from the recent Boer War. Different portions of the concession featured a British Army encampment, several South African native villages (including Zulu, San, and Swazi) and a 15-acre (61,000 m2) arena in which soldiers paraded, and major battles from the War were re-enacted, with over 600 veteran soldiers from both sides of the war. At the conclusion of the show, the Boer General Christian de Wet (portrayed by an actor of course) would escape on horseback by leaping from a height of 35 feet (11 m) into a pool of water. Another was "Battle Abbey" designed to be a 400 x 250 foot replica of the convent near Hastings, where the Normans defeated the Saxons. It was fashioned complete with towers, bastions, parapet, drawbridge. Inside was a museum of American wars with six huge cycloramas depicting famous American battles Gettysburg, Manassas, Yorktown, New Orleans, Buena Vista, Little Big Horn and Manila. The Gettysburg cyclorama was 50 feet high and 400 feet in circumference.

Geronimo St Louis 1904

Of the many exhibits that were at this fair, perhaps the saddest was Geronimo, Apache war chief. Once again (as was at the fairs in Omaha and Buffalo) he was placed, as Wikipedia called it "on display" in a tepee in the Ethnology Exhibit. He sold photographs for twenty-five cents, signed autographs for ten, fifteen, or twenty-five cents, as the case might be. Supposedly he got to keep part of the money, others claim he did not as he was still a prisoner of war and only let out of his Oklahoma jail to attend the fairs. "Many people in St. Louis invited Geronimo to come to their homes, but his `keeper' always refused. Every Sunday the President of the Fair sent the 74 year-old chief to go to the Wild West Show, where he took part in roping contests." He had

134

this to say about the whites, "I am glad I went to the Fair. I saw many interesting things and learned much of the white people. They are a very kind and peaceful people. During all the time I was at the Fair no one tried to harm me in any way. Had this been among the Mexicans, I am sure I should have been compelled to defend myself often. I wish all my people could have attended the Fair."[68] This sounds much what a prisoner let out of jail for a few months would say about the very people who allowed him time outside.

These fairs put primitive people on display. From a documentary on the St Louis World Fair one of the historians remarked, "Fairs were the celebration of Western Civilization, of its superior intellectual and scientific achievement. The firm belief was that if we could spread that around the world, everyone would be better off." Hence the primitives were shown off like animals at a zoo, who needed the great western industrialists and Christians to come save and fix them. Such displays included the Apache of the American Southwest and the Igorot of the Philippines, both of which peoples were dubbed as "primitive". "The Cliff Dwellers", was a reproduction of the caves of the Southwestern United States, covering over five acres of ground, containing over 100 dwellings and peopled by 300 natives of the Moki and Zuni races, including men, women and children. For an extra 25 cents one could enter the theater to watch Indians perform Snake and Kachina dances. One could purchase authentic baskets weaving, pottery and silver-work.

JW Buel wrote in the opening of his volume on Anthropology at the Exposition that the fairs, "has an all-embracing scope, in which is to be seen the works of men of all races, the primitive and the barbaric brought in contrast with the most highly civilized, that every step or progress may be observed."

One positive exhibit of note was for the horse Jim Key, the "educated" Arabian-Hambletonian cross horse in his Silver Horseshoe Pavilion. He was owned by Dr. William Key, an African-American/Native American former slave, who became a respected self-taught veterinarian. He took the horse on tour of the US to show his philosophy of humane treatment of animals, and to show that animals have feelings and thoughts, and not just things to work in field labour. Jim Key could add, subtract, use a cash register, spell with blocks, tell time and give opinions on the politics of the day by shaking his head yes or no. Dr. Key's motto was that Jim "was taught by kindness" instead of the whip.[69]

---

[68]From atthefair.com
[69]Wikipedia

The Fair hosted the 1904 Summer Olympic Games at the same time, the first Olympics held in the United States. These games had originally been awarded to Chicago, but when St. Louis threatened to hold a rival international competition, the games were relocated. Nonetheless, the sporting events, spread out over several months, were overshadowed by the Fair. With travel expenses high, many European athletes did not come. Many of the events were bogus, and the marathon turned out to be the strangest race maybe ever run, with the winner taking rat poison during the race, and another using a taxi cab to get the finish line first.

Then the fair was dismantled. The Chicago Wrecking Company won the contract, and had it dismantled in less than 2 years. All of the buildings, structures and statues were said to be buried in three landfills. I would love to see those landfills to see how much marble might still be in them. This fiar again lost money. A lot of money. Total cost 15 million, total return 6.4 million. Loss of 8.6 million (or 231,000,000 in todays money). They keep losing massinve amounts of money, yet they keep putting them on. Why you have to ask. Why indeed.

But strange is not the word as we head towards the Expo in San Francisco. That is because it was just 9 years after its great earthquake of 1906 made the city look like Hiroshima or Nagasaki. So yes the best thing one can do is put up 400 acres of buildings, to be used for only a few months, then tear them all down. Who needs housing and buildings after a completely devastating earthquake? Apparently not San Francisco. Or was it an earthquake?

CHAPTER 6
SAN FRANCISCO 1915

The next, and final fair to talk about is the 1915 Panama Exhibition in San Francisco. It was the last of the Great Fairs, and becomes the marker (with World War One) for what came historically before after. Prior to the First World War the fairs had an industrial theme, based around Greco-Roman buildings. After the War came more modern-style exposition buildings, and a focus on science and carnival type fun.

*

SAN FRANCISCO

The name for the state California was given to it when the Spanish owners believed (or may have at the time correctly understood) that California was an island. As such the area was named after the mythological island in a famous novel *Las Sergas de Esplandian* by Garci Rodriguez de Montalvo. In his book an island east of Asia was inhabited only by black Amazon-type women. The queen of the women was Califa, who was linked to a fortune of gold. California has become known as the "golden state." So is this from the "gold rush" of 1849, or was there something about gold and California that known long before that? Cities of lost gold west of the Mississippi were folklore on the American East Coast. They may not have been simple legends, but based on actual truth. Also don't forget 1960's this is the state of beach "California girls" culture. Something seems truly linked with the mythical 1400's novel, and the land that became known as American California. Perhaps it was not a mythical novel, but pointing to something much more real.

137

SAN FRANCISCO IN NOVEMBER,1848

What San Francisco is supposed to look like in 1848

The Spanish are claimed to have ventured to the area of San Francisco in 1769. Soldiers and a small group of settlers arrived in 1776- a coincidental date as it also the start of the US Revolution and signing Declaration of Independence. For some reason it seems that the date 1776 wants to be stamped in the head of the student of history and the start of anything in the USA. A fort (Presidio) and a Mission (Dolores) were built.

The new Spanish settlement was given the name Yerba Buena, supposedly meaning "good herbs" (reminding me of Chicago supposedly being named from onions). It became a trading center for visiting ships. Mexico gained its independence from Spain in the 1820's and took over California. In 1835, Englishman William Richardson built a house in Yerba Buena and set up a street plan for the new city. Of course in the standard historical narrative not one Spaniard or Mexican had thought of setting up a future street and city plan. It took a great and heroic "English person" to show up suddenly to do so. The Hudson's Bay Company opened a trading post 1841, and set up in what the Wikipedia article claims, "A large building on the water's edge was purchased." What large building? We have drawing of what the city is supposed to look like in 1848 above. Where is the large building that can be purchased n 1841? The trading post lasted a year then was closed and the HBC returned to Vancouver. What happened to the large building?

138

This next claim is important, "The settlement was arranged in the Spanish style around a plaza that remains as the present day Portsmouth Square." When you look again at the drawing of San Francisco in 1848, where is the supposed plaza? We will come back to that question shortly.

1846 becomes a very interesting year for San Francisco. It has a population of 800, a fort, a mission, and an unseen plaza. Firstly, North California was claimed by the US from Mexico in the Mexican-American War on July 7, supposedly without firing a shot. Sailors from the ship *Portsmouth* went into Yerba Buena and raised the American flag over the town plaza when the town offered no resistance. The name of the area was changed to that of ship, becoming Portsmouth Square. Just 3 weeks later, July 31, 1846, 240 Mormon migrants led by Sam Brannan arrive on the ship the *Brooklyn*. It seems very co-incidental to have them show up less than three weeks after one US navy ship captured the city. Why would they be coming to a Mexican city, because there could not have gotten everything together in less than three weeks. By January 30 1847 Yerba Buena had its name changed to San Francisco. This of course is odd because the new US settlers chose a Spanish name (Saint Francis) for a small town they had just captured. That makes no sense at all. English people like to name cities New York and New London and New Hampshire. So this Spanish name must have been a part of the city "long before" it became an American city.

In 1848 James Marshall is supposed to have found gold (again which was announced in Portsmouth Square), but took another year before the gold rush of 1849 began. In one year the population of the city was to rise from 1,000 to 25,000. The gold rush and Mormon arrival in 1846 do not on the surface seem linked. But they may be. *Weewarrior website* has found that Joseph Smith, the originator of the Mormon church came from "a family of *money diggers* who claimed they could locate treasure by looking at a stone in a hat." The Mormons also settled Salt Lake City in the 1850's, and then all of a sudden spectacular architecture springs up overnight. So WW speculates that Smith may have had some sort of knowledge or an ancient map as to where the old cities were (not using hats and stones), cities that included great treasures. The man credited with the California gold discovery, (James Marshall) was working for the leader of the Mormon settlers, Samuel Brannan, the one who arrived suddenly in 1846. In fact it was Brannan on May 12, 1848, who was the one to make headlines by running through the streets of San Francisco with a bottle full of gold- starting the actual gold rush. Brannan owned the store where all the mining supplies were purchased and made a "killing" in selling the supplies to the original gold diggers becoming the first millionaire in the state. The point of course was to give a reason to shift large numbers of population westward, to work in the gold and mercury mines, or other endeavors.

This photo is claimed to be San Francisco along Portsmouth Square 1851

By 1870 the city has a population of 150,000.[70] Ok that is quite a story. How true is it though? To go from 800 people to 150,000 in 30 years. Let us look a few things much closer, and this Portsmouth Square is going to be a central part of the investigation.

The above photo is what they want you to think San Francisco looked like in 1851 (and the very spot where the flag was raised in 1847), and would make sense to be given the history presented. But below is another photo from 1851, of the harbor. Where did all these buildings come from in four years? Because according to a very detailed article in sfmuseum.org this Plymouth Square was bustling long before 1850.

---

[70]History from San Francisco coming form sfmuseum.org, localhistories.org, hiddensf.com, and from the books on the San Francisco Exhibition such as *The Story of the Expostion, 1915*

San Francisco 1851 Harbor

While just about every historical article on San Francisco only focuses on Barbary Coast prostitute this, first Chinese person that, or the 1890 population, an article on sfmuseum focuses on Portsmouth Square in 1850. First the article claims there was a giant Customs House. But more importantly were a series of great hotels, "a line of palaces, the magnificence of whose interior even more than corresponds to the promise as their outward show. They were all devoted to the fickle goddess, Fortune, but they are good lounges for one who can withstand temptation." One was the Parker House, first built in the spring of 1849. It was 65 feet long along the Square, and 145 feet in depth, two stories high. Where is this structure in the photo of the Square two images above? What is the history of these hotels? Oh yes, like all cities everything important gets burned in a fire and had to be rebuilt. The hotel was rebuilt 4 times. Why? Because history claims that early San Francisco went through five massive city fires (Jan 4 1849, Dec 24 1849, May 4 1850, June 14 1850, September 17 1850). Each time the hotels and the all the buildings were rebuilt. Only to have it all burn down again. At least that is the story, but then we have the painting (lithograph) below of the Square in 1850 and it is very damning to the official historical story.

Lithograph by John Prendergast, 1850 of the statehood celebration in Plymouth Square

Take a close look at this drawing. That is supposed to be the same Portsmouth Square in the photograph above from 1851. Notice anything odd? How about the Parthenon looking building on the left? Or the giant columned structure further beyond. Who was building this in/by 1849 when standard history claims shacks and 1000 people? Why are none of these buildings appearing in the 1851 Portsmouth Square image? If everything was getting destroyed in fires, how could any of the buildings from the lithograph burn down because quite clearly they are made of brick and stone and not wood? What is the real story of Portsmouth Square, where the city was captured in war, gold was announced, statehood celebrated, and where great hotels stood- but then we are given a "cowboy looking" 1851 photograph. Yet the lithograph looks like downtown Athens. So which is true? What is the real story of the growth of San Francisco?

I must stop the flow of the book, to place seven images together on the next two pages. What they are is the divided photos of a complete panoramic view photographed in 1878. Take a look at San Francisco.

The San Francisco panoramas of 1878 by Eadweard Muybridge

This might be one of the most shocking pieces of photographic evidence out there. What you are looking at is a panorama of San Francisco claimed to have been taken in 1878.[71] It was taken by Eadweard Muybridge (the same man who later gave a moving picture display at the 1893 Chicago Exposition). Look at the size of the city. There might be half a million people there. Look at the buildings- huge towers, domes, facades, beautiful architecture, a Cathedral that would fit right in Central Moscow. Can that really be built in less than 30 years? With all the ornate finish of the roofs and column mansions, after having started with a city of just miners and cowboys? I don't think so, and neither does my building contractor friend. The amount of manpower and machine power needed would be enormous unless a) they had technology they were not supposed to have, or b) much of that city was already there long ago. There is no other answer. The gold rush may have been a fabricated story to get people to move real fast from east to west, and start filling up these mostly empty cities they had just found in California. This panorama is actually very destructive evidence to the standard historical narrative.

There is more strangeness in the panorama. No construction work of any kind is going on. Everything everywhere is finished. This is supposed to be a booming city, with thousands moving there every day. Wouldn't there be a need to be building something, somewhere? Even more spooky, is that there are no people, no horses no nothing. Ok a few, maybe 50 horse and carts and 100 people. The clock tower shows 12.30, so it mid day. Where are all the people? The standard explanation is that early cameras had to take ten minute exposures so the photographer kept people out of photos. Really, they could keep 200,000 people, and 50,000 horses out of a photo for ten minutes. There would have to be a ton of blurring in the photos from people and horses moving around. But there is no blurring. Lets be clear, there are almost no people in this city when this panorama was taken. We see these similar city photos all over the world during this time period 1860-1880. A complete city, with no work being done, and no people to be found anywhere.

I think we are looking at a city at the edge of being taken over, "found dead", "dis covered", some "free masonry." This might be a photo

---

[71]This panorama can be seen at Wikipedia and can be zoomed into very close detail of all of the buildings.
https://commons.wikimedia.org/wiki/File:Panorama_of_San_Francisco_by_Eadweard_Muybridge,_1878.jpg

the day the resettlement began, not some 20 years after being founded with log cabins by some cowboys and miners. The drawing we have of Portsmouth Square indicates that San Francisco is not what was normally presented at this period. What were historians doing during time frame? If this was all true, why was no one reporting it?

*

1894 FAIR

San Francisco 1894, Mechanical Building and Tower (that would be dynamited in 1896)

While the San Francisco Fair of 1915 will be our focus, few people know that this was actually the earlier major fair in that city in 1894 on the heels of the end of the one in Chicago.[72] The 1894 fair opened on January 27 and took place in Golden Gate Park. It ended on July 4. The idea came from Chicago Exposition commissioner Michael H. de Young who thought (as the country to was going through a giant recession) that a fair in California would help to stimulate the economy. Now of course to me this seems like more of a money grab for him than anything else. Here he was in charge of the Chicago Expo, the biggest money maker and propaganda creator anyone had ever seen. He had

[72] San Francisco also had a fair in 1909 called the Portolo Festival. Only 1 or 2 photos seem to exist and they do not show any buildings.

146

all of these people from all over the world setting up midway exhibits, and I think the idea was to convince some of them to stay and just ship the show (in a smaller version) to San Francisco. Of course why specifically San Francisco and not Los Angeles is a question. But there were issues. Golden Gate Park Superintendent John McLaren had no interest in a fair in his park stating "the damage to the natural setting would take decades to reverse." Even over McLaren's great objections the fair was built.

It seems a new construction record was reached. Bancroft's Fair book adds a chapter on the 1894 Fair and wrote, *"Not least among the wonders of the 1894 Exposition was the speed with which its structures were erected...it may be said that, like the city which contains them, they sprang up almost in a night. It was not until late in September that the contracts for the first buildings were awarded, and yet at the formal opening on the 27th of January, a space of about four months, all the principal and most of the minor pavilions were practically completed. While none of them rival the magnificent proportions of the Columbian temples, there are many whose skillful composition and beauty of design leave nothing to be desired."* The fair encompassed 200 acres, 120 structures were built, and more than 2 million people visited. Like all other fairs, most of the buildings were torn down after the event. So all of that was done in 4 months time *"almost overnight"*. Two hundred acres and one hundred and twenty giant buildings in four months. Reminded many times in the passage that they sprung up "almost in a night" just "like the city which contains them." This metaphorical presentation of the fairs going up as if magical power was used is a symbol again and again in the books of the period.

The Administration Building featured a 135-foot-tall dome with figures in relief. The Agriculture/Horticulture Building featured three domes to let in light for the plants. The 266 feet high Bonet Tower was a large steel tower set in the center of the Grand Court of Honor that used electrical lighting. It was approximately a third the size of the Eiffel Tower, after which it was modeled. The tower was adorned with 3,200 multicolored lights, and the upper level of the tower had a spotlight. Bancroft wrote, "In the illumination of the Fair the Electric Tower is the principal feature; for here is one of the most powerful search-lights in the world, its comet-like rays distinctly visible more than 50 miles at sea." This may mean what it seems it does, or could be a reference that the Tower in fact was the "principle feature" in making the electricity, not in presenting it. The tower stayed for 2 years after the fair until McLaren had it destroyed with high-powered explosives. Yes explosives.

The Fine Arts Building was "an Egyptian revival structure," surmounted with the likeness of Hathor. The building itself was a brick structure built 50 feet high with a small pyramid on top. After the Midwinter Exposition ended, it remained (as it was an "intended permanent structure") and became The Fine Arts Museum. The 1906 earthquake apparently ruined the integrity of the building, which led to closure for repairs. It was not destroyed or vaporized like the rest of the city, just suffered some structural damage. In 1929 the building was finally torn down.

The Manufactures and Liberal Arts Building (170,000 square feet) featured many displays from the Columbian Exhibition in Chicago, which against tends to me to believe that this was just a do it again quick kind of venture. Like Chicago there were the ethnic villages: Eskimo, African, and the popular Cairo Street (of course). The Santa Barbara Amphibia was an exhibit that held many species of marine life that made the Santa Barbara channel their home. Basically a giant aquarium, it was faced with a giant pyramid there with Egyptian facing.

After the fair McLaren made sure to have all of the fair destroyed from the park. Why he kept the Fine Arts Building (that with its Egyptian look) and the Japanese Village, along with multiple statues is not adequately explained.

EARTHQUAKE 1906

Locals watch as the city burns, 1906

We have seen that like Chicago and St Louis, San Francisco had its shares of city destroying fires in the 1800's. But this city goes one better on the destruction scale, the earthquake of 1906. I mean we have lots of photographs and had witnesses about that disaster. Surely that must be as history states. Well the earthquake story is quite strange too once it gets examined.

The first oddity is that there is video of it, well sort of. The first video is a trip down the main street (from a cable car) taken just four days before the quake. How lucky! The entire video seems staged based on what the cars, wagons and people in front are doing. Basically it is a Hollywood film of a street line car ride in San Francisco. Ok, but then the 7.9 quake comes on April 18 that leads to a series of firestorms being created (as happened in Chicago and the other destroyed cities of the period) that lasted at least two days. Four days after the quake another video is taken, on seemingly the same cable car, going down the same street. How convenient. What is odd when watching that second video (you can see both on youtube) how calm the people are that are walking around. Basically the entire city has been destroyed, loved one and animals killed and badly injured, yet everyone is walking

149

around like they are headed to watch a football game. It makes it all more odd.

Odd actions of the people on Sacramento Street April 18,1906, especially those on chairs in the foreground.

When you look at photos taken during the fire (and there are lots of them such as the one above) the people just seem odd. There are hundreds of people on the streets, all watching the event, and they are dressed in their best clothes as if they are on their way to church and just stopped to enjoy a view of the fire before heading off to get their hair cut. They are not all behaving like a city in the midst of an earthquake causing to city to be burning all around them. There is even a group of guys on the right side just sitting on chairs causally watching the city burn. Huh? Move out some belongings. Help an old person or children get to safety. No here they just sit and watch the city burn down while they eat lunch. And this is not the only photo of its kind. The thought that keeps coming to mind with this is movie extras.

Selfies by women taking during the San Francisco fire

How about this odd photo. It is a group of women high on a hill, getting their "selfie" taken with a burning city in the background. Why would they be so happy and joyous. That makes no sense. Are they time travelers? Some group involved in creating the disaster? Just sick psychopaths? Or is something else going on here? It is almost feels like to me all the people in these photos, are just like the people in the videos from the street car. Actors. For actors do this on movie sets- take pics with the stars, or the "set" they are working on. I see them as people paid to be there and make it look like something is happening. But what is happening? Was there really an earthquake?

Some San Francisco Earthquake photos

How about the photos of the destruction itself. Go look at more yourself on the internet. In the top photo the city is basically crushed- yet again the utility poles are all standing fine. What actually does that kind of damage? Direct bombardment by a battleship, bombs from a B-29? Interestingly the Roman pillars and the giant dome seems to make it through. But the next photo is very problematic.

San Francisco two weeks after the quake

This is supposed to be taken a few weeks after the earthquake, in May 1906. First off look at the damage. It appears as though 90% of

152

this part of the city is wiped out. Again that looks like the site of WW2 bombing raid. Yes earthquakes can be devastating, we have all seen them on newscasts in our lifetime. But I don't think I have ever seen images of basically an entire city looking like it has been nuked from an earthquake. Secondly and more odd, where is all the rubble of the collapsed structures here? You can not clean up the remains of 10,000 destroyed buildings in a few weeks. It took even years to clean up after the collapse of the World Trade Center in New York, and that is with the best modern equipment. Horse crews could not clean up an entire city after an earthquake this fast. This city looks vaporized, and I don't think a giant fire alone can do that. What is more odd is how most of the WOODEN utility poles (electricity or wireless internet or whatever they are) seem to make it through the fires just fine. So what happened? When did it happen? It is also claimed that San Francisco could burn so fast (like all the other fire cities) was because all the buildings were made of wood. Yet look close at the 1878 panorama again in chapter 3. There are a few wood buildings there, but like Chicago most are brick and stone. Something is just not right with these city destruction stories. Can we get some other clues about this?

The odd Aggazi Statue at Stanford University just after the quake

This photo above is of a statue "damaged" in the earthquake. What are the odds a statue could crash through the stone street like this? This is very clearly a staged photo. Why? What is the message? The statue is of Louis Aggazi who was a key professor of biology and geology at Harvard University from just after his arrival to the US in 1847 until his death in 1873. He was also the founder of the Museum of Comparative Zoology, and was one of the first scientists to claim that there had been an Ice Age on earth. His was most famous for being the staunch resister to the ideas of Darwin's Evolution. It was why he lost his credibility with the scientific community just before his death. Science buried him and his ideas just like the way the statue is depicted. A key in the complete photo is that word Zoology above the door is clearly centered in the shot. Symbolically it is saying that Aggazi had burying his head in the sand, as anyone else also not believing in Darwin and the greatness of the new ruling elite. Symbolism personified. So why do this after a city destroying earthquake. Would not everyone have much more to do with basic survival than how to dig out a street to make a symbolic photo? Again it is hard to know just what was going on in April 1906/

A researcher from stolenhistory.org (minlo66)[73] located a series of documents from 1906 that can be seen on the sfmuseum.net website. Without going into all the details here, the basic overview is that a series of army corps engineers were using dynamite on buildings just after the earthquake. It describes the days April 18 and 19 when "buildings were blown up far enough ahead of the fire to avoid feeding the fire with flying embers and to effectually stop the fire for lack of fuel, by cutting a broad open belt ahead of the fire." So this is claiming that buildings were being blown up on purpose to stop the fire from, you know, destroying the buildings. That sounds odd. He then provides the name of all the brave men involved in the operation, and that they should be given special commendation by the Military for their service on these days.

Is this true, or simply just a very nice explanation to explain the ruins of buildings that could not be explained by simple fire alone? Or were buildings dynamited without there having been a city fire? A second letter found at the sfmuseum site sent from Benj. I. Wheeler of the University of California to President Taft on July 24, 1906, discussing a different letter sent by UOC professor H Morse Stephens asking to

---

[73]Entire thread of information around this topic can be read in who nuked San Francisco, specifically page 3.

see the complete report by General Greely. Wheeler's letter states, "*Dear Secretary Taft: The enclosed letter implies a request which I deem reasonable and worthy. Professor Stephens is a first-rate historical scholar and withal a man of rare tact and good judgment. He is making up the story of the disaster and its relief as a sample of the proper type of historical investigation. You can trust absolutely to his discretion and wisdom. Faithfully yours,*" So what exactly is this letter suggesting regarding Stephens "making up the story of the disaster"? Does that mean that he is working on documenting the moment by moment details for posterity, or that he is in charge of making it up- as in fabricating a false story? It is speculation based on the wording of the document, but I thought it needed to be added to this examination.

SF listed as "two years after"

San Francisco 1909

Next come the above two odd photographs. Well they don't seem odd at first glace, just pictures of San Francisco after having rebuilt the city. It is the time frame in these photos. They are photos in 1908 and 1909. You have seen the earthquake disaster photos above, where basically nothing was left. How can in two years a complete build of all the brick and stone buildings we see in these photographs happen? It is just not possible.[74] Could anyone believe that San Francisco had been totally rebuilt in two years? Or was the city in 1908 fine, and been fine all along? Because it was not fully built in two years, and be shown with again with zero construction happening in the photographs. So that either means one of two things (a) if there was a disaster in San Francisco, it must have been a long time ago (at least 100 or 200 years) and was photographed at the time (meaning photography is much older than claimed) and then the city was fully built up over those hundreds of years to give us the images such as the 1878 panorama and the photos above. Thus the earthquake of 1906 was some sort of "forged" event using the photos of the long ago disaster, and the Hollywood type actors were hired to create scenes like it occurred in 1906. Or (b) there was no disaster at any time to San Francisco, and in 1906 perhaps a small part of the city was purposely destroyed (say with dynamite). That area was photographed from

---

[74] I saw the same image in a 1908 drawing. That year a giant fleet of US warships traveled the world (on some sort of odd presentation of peace). It was known as the Great White Fleet, and one of the stops of the fleet was in San Francisco. Ok it was coming to bring hope to the damaged city. What kind of peace mission in a foreign land should have you dock 16 battleships in their port? Sort of like Orwellian doublespeak, was the "peace" mission really a disguised war mission? Or was it some sort of war like victory lap of the world?

several angles to suggest the entire city was like this one area. It then becomes easy to rebuild ten or twenty blocks of a city in 2 or so years, because the rest of the city was just fine. With either scenario, because of the belief of a destroyed city in an earthquake there will be no question of the age of the buildings (has to be after 1906). I am leaning to a/b) here, that something happened to San Francisco a long time in the past, and it was just pasted over to pretend to have happened in 1906.

Another oddity is a 1908 (co-incidentally the same year as these other photos) photo of an Elk's Club meeting in San Francisco. Unfortunately this one was found by a photographer at a local garage sale, and I can not print it, but you can look at it here.[75] The elite are gathering, and obviously happily living it up and partying. This while much of the city is supposed to be still living in refugee camps and barely functioning slums (which of course we don't see in main photos). These people in the Elks Club photo don't have a care in the world. This very image reminds me of the closing shot of Kubrick's masterpiece The Shining, a movie that links later with Eyes Wide Shut to present the control of the masses, and who it is that is doing the controlling. That party and this party, hence the message coming from Kubrick is all in the same.

SF City Hall, built 1913

---

[75] https://www.ronhenggeler.com/History/elks_club.htm

Above is the look of San Francisco's post earthquake rebuild, because what every city needs right after an earthquake when no one has anywhere to sleep at night besides tents is to build monoliths like this above. And you should look inside the City Hall to see magnificence even more than the exterior. Then they hold a fair in 1909, The Portolo Festival. While there are not many photos of this fair, mainly the starting parade, there are a lot of posters from it. The are all odd.[76] A Spanish-looking Women cuddling a bear overlooking the city, or a Spanish-looking woman walking down some Greek steps surrounded by roses.

No matter, the presentation being made after 1906 is that San Francisco, just like Chicago was, is a phoenix rising out of the ashes to bring a beautiful new world to everyone's day to day lives. Of course again all the main building needs to emulate Ancient Rome.

*

1915 Panama-Pacific Exhibition

Birds Eye View of 1915 Exhibition

That brings us to the 1915 Panama–Pacific International Exposition of San Francisco, to celebrate the completion of the Panama Canal. It began on February 20- but the exposition was as much to show off the city's amazing recovery from the earthquake. *"When the Panama-Pacific International Exposition opened in 1915, San Francisco*

---

[76]https://calisphere.org/item/8882717c4cb714551229d6adafaa06f1/

looked fabulous: Bedecked with ornate, European-inspired architecture and an array of technological wizardry, the city resumed its role as a West Coast powerhouse less than a decade after near-total destruction. Block after block of property flattened by the 1906 earthquake and ensuing fires had been transformed to make way for glitzy new hotels, sturdy apartment buildings, landscaped parks and courtyards, offices, theaters, and a sparkling, gold-topped City Hall. New streetcar lines were built to carry visitors and locals to the fair, much of which rose on previously uninhabitable lots along the city's northern waterfront. The Panama-Pacific International Exposition showed the world that the city had reached new heights of grandeur, launching the modern incarnation of San Francisco like a phoenix from the ashes."[77]

Like Chicago they also chose a swamp area, today known as the Marina District. The fair was constructed on a 636 acre (2.6 km2) site between the Presidio and Fort Mason. Before the fair it was supposed to be a small 400-property neighborhood known as Harbor View. The buildings were all claimed to have been demolished to make the fair grounds. But as Laura Ackerly wrote in her 2015 book, there was collusion about it. Though nearly a hundred earthquake refugee shacks had been located in Harbor View, their owners were evicted after their homes were condemned by the Department of Health. But of course they only condemned the shacks in the Harbour View area, nowhere else in the city. Wikipedia claims "76 city blocks had been cleared or filled to set the stage for the exposition." So why would the area need to be cleared if an earthquake and fire had basically destroyed the city? And if they did spend a great amount of time and energy to build things on those sites AFTER AN EARTHQUAKE, why would you then tear them all down, to build temporary structures, to tear those down, and build something else again?

---

[77] *Tower of Jewels* By Hunter Oatman-Stanford —Collectors Weekly March 27th, 2015, and   Laura Ackley, *San Francisco's Jewel City: The Panama-Pacific International Exposition of 1915*

159

Photos captioned "laying out the exhibition grounds"

Let us talk a bit about the building of this fair, as this one has the most photographs to date besides St Louis. Many of the photos are of temporary wood buildings. Now of course that does not mean there were also permanent buildings there that were just ignored in the photographs. Fine you say again they wanted staged photos with just a few men to show off the buildings...but with a workforce of 20,00 there would be signs of them around. A cup left on the ground somewhere, a half of a sandwich, some nails, a hammer sitting along something. However the ground is barren is barren of any semblance of work in the staged photos.

FRAMING THE PALACE OF MANUFACTURES

The book *Story of the Exposition (5 volumes)* by Frank Morton Todd put out in 1921 by Putnam and Sons and available online has many construction photos in the second volume. And it is quite clear that certainly many of the buildings are just what they say they are. Wood structures including iron and steel truss roofs. In fact there is more steel going into these buildings than I have seen any fair prior to this one save Chicago. But this fair also produces another problem when looking carefully at many of the buildings. That is the show of weathering. Long time weathering. So how are buildings supposed to show 50 or 100 years of weathering if they have just been put up one year previously? Again is this a fair of Ancient Rome personified, or Ancient Rome dug out and re-presented as new?

161

Poster for 1915, with "Columbia" depicted among ruins similar to Ancient Rome, while overlooking the Exposition

On top of that, over 30 countries sent exhibits to the fair...while there was World War 1 going on! Granted Britain and Germany withdrew and sent no exhibits, however France still did. No one seemed to concerned about shipping expensive exhibits and priceless art across the Atlantic...in the middle of the biggest war the world had ever known. A war that included German submarine attacks in the open waters.

California Building today, San Diego

Oh and there wasn't just a Worlds Fair in SF...no no, there was another similar one going on just south in San Diego at the same time. And San Diego seems not to have torn down many of their buildings but kept many such as the California Building (with its dome), California Tower and the current Museum of Art (with its statue lined front facade).

Time to look at the finished product in San Francisco.

163

San Francisco 1915

Look at the structures in San Francisco. Hundreds of buildings, domes, columns, statues, lagoons. The exposition was sometimes referred to as "The Domed City," because of the many buildings with dome tops, including the Palace of Fine Arts, Festival Hall, the Manufacturers Palace, Liberal Arts Palace, the Palace of Horticulture and the Palace of Varied Industries. The buildings had a very strict eight color pastel theme that had to be adhered to, so that the overall effect was one of complete unity between the buildings.

The Tower of Jewels was the 435 foot tall centerpiece building of the Exhibition. Emily Post described the building as "a diamond and turquoise wedding cake." It was taller than the other fair buildings by a couple hundred feet, and was positioned at the main Scott Street entrance to the fair. It was covered with over 100,000 cut glass Novagems, which sparkled in sunlight throughout the day and were illuminated by over 50 powerful electrical searchlights at night. "Made in Bohemia, the Novagems came in several colors of glass and were mounted on brass hangers with a small mirror behind them to further increase their reflecting. As these jewels freely hung from the sides of the building, the breezes would make them independently sway, causing the building to shimmer in a way that people say was impossible to describe unless one saw it in person." Inside were a variety of large painted murals, depicting allegorical scenes of such things as Balboa discovering the Pacific Ocean and the progress of the Panama Canal.

On a few special occasions, they put on an event known as "Burning the Tower" where (according to Todd's, *The Story of the Exposition*), "Concealed ruby lights, and pans of red fire behind the colonnades on the different galleries, seemed to turn the whole gigantic structure into a pyramid of incandescent metal, glowing toward white heat and about to melt. From the great vaulted base to the top of the sphere, it had the unstable effulgence of a charge in a furnace, and yet it did not melt, however much you expected it to, but stood and burned like some sentient thing doomed to eternal torment." The lighting director for the Fair was Walter D'Arcy Ryan, who had worked for General Electric. Ryan used new techniques to light up all the buildings of the fair. "In the Court of the Universe, Ryan concealed 1,500-watt lamps inside the decorative glass columns rising from the two central fountains—by day they appeared to be sculpted from marble but at night they transformed into bright beams of light. In the Court of Abundance, real flames burned in the mouths of sculpted snakes, while an 18-foot glass sphere in the Fountain of Earth utilized carefully placed interior lighting to imitate the effect of a massive rotating globe. Throughout the grounds, the evening ambiance was manipulated with carefully placed spotlights, softly glowing flames held aloft by statues, and bulbs concealed behind banners and other architectural details."[78]

The Palace of Machinery was the largest building on the grounds, and had all sorts of exhibits showing modern America's heavy machinery, machine tools, steam, gas and oil engines, passenger elevators and hoisting apparatuses, as well as electrical exhibits by Westinghouse and Edison. Inside the Palace of Horticulture's glass dome, the so-called Electric Kaleidoscope projected images of comets, sunsets, and fluttering spots resembling butterflies, waving ribbons, and other shapes. Every state in the Union had a building representing them at the exposition. Some states designed traditional conservative buildings, while some tried to use more of a flair for the original by designing buildings that conveyed a sense of what their state represented. For example, Oregon's state building was a replica of the Parthenon -- but instead of Greek marble pillars, they substituted 48 huge redwood trunks, one representing each state in the Union. Virginia's building was a reproduction of George Washington's home at Mt. Vernon, and included many pieces of furniture used by President Washington.

---

[78]Oatman

Area called the Court of the Universe, day and night views

There were 30,000 imported plants, trees, bushes and flowers including 70,000 rhododendrons. The landscape architect for this fair was none other than John McLaren, yes the John MCLaren who so hated the 1894 fair that had the tower dynamited when it was over. But now all of a sudden he is Mr. Fair. He needs to be more closely looked at as well. A telephone line was also established to New York City so people across the continent could hear the Pacific Ocean. The Liberty Bell traveled by train on a nationwide tour from Philadelphia, Pennsylvania, to attend the exposition. A five acre scale model of the Panama Canal was built, and the way it was painted gave the impression as if seeing the entire thousand mile real Canal. Another big exhibit was a simulated ride over Arizona's Grand Canyon.

Manufacturing was a key for this fair. The automobile was key and ford had an assembly line set up that produced 18 new cars every day of the fair, ended by being driven off the line. But it was more than this. All sorts of new assembly line items were down making products before people's eyes such as fire hoses and blue jeans. New airplanes were taking passengers for tours for the very high cost of $10 fee ten dollars. "The concession was run by two brothers whose last name was spelled 'Loughead.' Although they had already gone broke at least once they re-founded the Lockheed Aircraft Corporation using their profits from the fair."[79]

What author Ackely also makes clear in her book is that even though this was now the era of the car, and the car was being

---

[79]One stunt pilot died during the fair, his plane not coming out of a show spin he was doing, crashing into the Pacific.

showcased, "You had this modern fair, but horses and mules were critical to building it." So again she, and other historians are following the basic premise that even though machines were available, they still had all the lumber dragged by horses.

Again this was an expensive ticket. Granted the admission was only 50 cents, the problem was that to do anything cost money. Take a ride on the midway, money. Buy food, money. Take a train ride, money. Though many still try to portray that the average person could attend (due to the fair entrance only costing 50 cents) that meant the poor could go, but not do or eat anything.

Teardown of an obvious wooden structure

Palace of Fine Arts today

As soon as the fair came to a close, the demolition began. It took far less time to tear down this fair than did Chicago, St. Louis or the others. Supposedly a campaign started to save the Palace of Fine Arts. The building survived well into the 1960's, until it went through a complete reconstruction. Now again why did they choose to save just one building, and just how temporary was the structure if it made it fine into the 1960's. Then again San Diego had no problem keeping its fair buildings (the only fair city since 1851 to have done so) Again I would love to have had a very close inspection of the other buildings on site to see if they were all made from temporary wood and staff, or if hard marble and granite could be spotted on several.

Where did all the ruined buildings actually go? The story claims for St Louis, for example, that the remains of the fair (all 1200 acres of it) was dumped into three landfills. What landfills? Do you have an idea just how much "garbage" 1200 acres of massive buildings would produce? Any landfill site would be huge. Where are they? I wonder if there really are landfills or if something else may have happened to all the "now garbage" structures at the end of these fairs.

*

FAIRS TO THE PRESENT

The fairs stopped altogether after the San Francisco fair, the War being blamed as the main reason for the shut down. Though it took a

168

long time to get them up and running again, and when they did start again in the 1930's, they were nothing like they used to be. Fun and entertainment replaced history and artwork- flashy new "modern" buildings replaced the Greco-Roman style. This change has become even more prominent today. Now a sort of Utopian presentation focuses on outer space, AI, and VR technology. Only nine corporations had pavilions at 1893 Chicago, while by 2000 almost every exhibit is "corporate" sponsored. In effect showing that corporations now run everything. Now rather than trust that progress would come only from white people, the presentation began to shift in the 1950's that it would be science and governments that would solve all of humanity's problems. The early fairs were all about inustry and modernizing the savages, now to display that science is the new great religion. The more recent fairs have had ecology and saving the environment as key presentations, which is ironic given that many of the first fairs were all about how to control and force nature to do what humans (rather elite ruling humans) wanted it to do in order to make them a lot of money.

The most recent World Exposition was in Milan in 2015, the next for Dubai in 2020 with a theme of "Connecting Minds, Creating the Future." I have of course checked out a number of these modern Expos, and while large and somewhat unique, they just can not hold themselves to the size, scale and building opulence that was Chicago, St Louis, Paris or San Francisco. Ancient Rome was shown to be right in front of our nose...and perhaps it was- and is still. The cities were all part of the Roman Empire, and the Expos (particularly in the US) were modeled after two specific places...The Domus Aurea (Golden House of Nero) and Hadrian's Villa.

CHAPTER 7
Mudflood Terms

You might think of this as an extended glossary, providing detail on the words and terms being used by the current alternate historical community. This does not mean I agree with everything, but that I want to lay out background of the theories behind the words you will see being used- not only for reading this book, but also to help should you choose to do further research of your own. The first term that needs to be defined is "alternate history" itself.

*

ALTERNATE HISTORY

The term "alternate history previously was applied to specific fiction writers who used historical events, but added a twist to them (such as Germany invades and captures England in 1940, or John Kennedy does not die in 1963). While these provide interesting reading, this is not what is being referred to here.

This term has now being mostly used to refer to the theories of Anatoly Fomenko, a Russian mathematician and statistician. He developed a theory (that he called the New Chronology) that history was greatly misinterpreted after working in Soviet intelligence in the 1970's studying Western newspapers for misinterpretations. He was not the first to have these ideas. One of the early originators of this theory was Jean Hardouin[80] a French Jesuit scholar in the late 17th century. In his *Chronologiae Ex Nummis Antiquis Restitutae* of 1696 he claimed that *"with the exception of the works of Homer, Herodotus and Cicero, the Natural History of Pliny, the Georgics of Virgil, and the Satires and Epistles of Horace, all the rest of the ancient classics of Greece and Rome were manufactured (forged) by Benedictine monks."*[81] From reading similar theories, Fomenko published several 7-800 page volumes of his Chronology. Its core is to present a historical timeline that

---

[80] Hardouin however must be carefully examined, for he was a Jesuit scholar, who were likely one of the main groups behind the falsification of history itself. Thus was Hardouin and his presentation a part of that falsification (hiding something while pretending to call history out)- or did he gain actual knowledge in inner circles and tried to expose it in his lifetime? This question must be kept in mind.

[81] Wikipedia, Hardouin page

is much shorter than normal history, with the majority of historical events (from the Middle Ages to Ancient Egypt) falling in the period of our AD 1000–1500. While I agree with this basic premise that there are major problems with the standard historical timeline, I personally do not agree with his "revised" presentation. In fact I think it could be rather dangerous (such as claiming Napoleon's French army built the Egyptian pyramids). Many in the revisionist historical community are still are using his timeline and events as 100% factual, and this might be causing as much confusion as clarity.

Before getting into why I discredit much of what he presents, I do want to start with part of his theory that seems the most intriguing. That is his claim that 1000 years was added to history in the 1500's. Let me present to you how this likely happened.

The Council of Trent (1545-1563) in Northern Italy is presented has having occurred because the Vatican had a meeting to decide on a response to the rise of Protestantism. This council is supposed to have clarified scripture, original sin, doctrine, and a response. Yet the most important decision to come out if it tends to be ignored.[82] This was a decision to change the current Julian Calendar to standardize Easter by fixing a slight error in the calendar itself, and it might have been the Protestant response they decided upon. It took until 1582 to have this finally happen (which is a long time to just improve a calendar), when Pope Gregory (whom the current calendar we use is named after) supposedly added 10 days to the old calendar to fix the sun year at 365.25 days in his new one, while adding leap years, all to have Easter standardized. What is the problem you ask?

One of the greatest scams in history may have just taken place. The Council of Trent may not have been happening in 1545 AD but in year 545 of the Julian Calendar, there was no AD or BC yet. It took until 582 to finalize the change to the calendar because there was more than just a 365.24 day system being adopted. Actually 1000 years was also being added, to set up the entire structure for the new control of everything by the Vatican. People went to sleep on Sunday, October 4, 582 AD in the Julian Calendar and then woke up to Friday, October 15, 1582 on the new Gregorian Calendar without even knowing a switch was made, because it took a few more decades to finalize the switch.

---

[82] The wikipedia page of the Council does not have the calendar information, but it does appear on the Gregorian Calendar page

Why was the change needed? One reason was claimed to pass over the people's literal belief that Jesus would rise again in the year 1000. This way the Church could pass by the lead up to the date, and simply claim it never happened, which means "He" must have handed over all authority to the Church. Yet the more important reason, and the likely real one, was also for control. It was to create a false history for the Catholic Church, which in fact never existed. If you just added 1000 years of time, you had to have a history for those 1000 years. There was now a time period 583-1581 that did not actually exist, but needed to be created. And it would be the Vatican, and their personal police force (the Jesuits) who would write it. The best way to give yourself 1000 years of authority, is just make up the 1000 years with you at the center of it.[83]

Strange date on the old city Hall in Oslo Norway: 1641 or J641

---

[83] Thus the Church might only be in truth as much as 500 years old, even less, and the New Testament, at least in the form we know it in, might be from the same period of time. It seems there was a type of Christ figure (who that might be is unclear at this point)- but the story as we know it might be quite recent, and linked to this entire calendar change. Why is there is no actual historical record of a person named Jesus in the Middle East by the historians writing at the the time 0-50 AD. The name only appears many years later. Other key figures were recorded in the histories. That is because there likely was no such person. He was an invention of the church (based on a real figure from the past) who became the main hero in similar mythology all over the world (Osiris, Dyanosis, Mithras, Krishna).

The change was not made right after the Council of Trent in 1545, for it seems time was needed to lay the foundation in place that it would require. Monks were instructed to start using a small j or small "i" prior to a date. So 550 would be written j550 for example. The j or "i" indicating the year of Jesus or year of Iasus. This addition was quickly followed in all parts of the Catholic world (even in most Protestant areas). The next part of the trick happened a few decades later when the small letters were changed to a large J or large I, as seen in the date in the photo above on the Old City Hall in Oslo, Norway. Historians claim this date is 1641, but it is quite clearly can not be as the two supposed 1's are of completely different style. The first on is a J the second is a 1. This is the year Jesus 641. But within one hundred years, all the J's and I's would be believed to be a 1000 placeholder.

By the early J600's the Vatican began having priests replace the J or I with a 1 and make what would have been I622 into 1622. It seems like a simple letter to number change but it is much much greater. The creation of 1000 years of time was now complete. Many Protestant countries rejected the calendar change, and vehemently also rejected the date writing change, which is why we see the J and I in dates for the longest period of time in Protestant European countries (such as Norway and Germany). But the 1000 millennium could now pass with no savior having returned, the Church had taken total control with a made up history, and then began a process of integrating with new formed groups called Freemasons and the Illuminati to control every aspect of Western religion, government, commerce, and law. It all come directly out of this calendar change.

The question becomes just how much of history was falsified, almost all of it (as someone like Fomenko believes) or simply parts of it as I believe. The premise is that events were duplicated, presented as happening in different parts of the world in different years. Ever wonder why there were massacres in France in the 1200's of Cathars, then again in the 1300's of Knights Templar? They were both connected groups, perhaps even the same group. So why only kill off one half while leaving the other half. It is quite likely there was only one series of massacres, and they all happened at the same time. Of course what year that actually took place is almost impossible now to know.

The normal historical timeline that we have come to believe, is claimed by Fomenko to have mostly been manufactured by Joseph Justus Scaliger in Opus Novum de emendatione temporum (1583), which interestingly comes out right at the exact time of the calendar shift mentioned as well as the Galileo's heliocentric response. However Scaliger was a Protestant and his work greatly angered the Jesuits, who wanted to lay claim to being the center of all knowledge and research. Scaliger's historical chronology was completed in 1627 by the Jesuit Dionysus Petavius, creating the AD-BC system we still use today. The Jesuits have long been what might be called the secret police force of the Vatican, and when something needs "hushing," "tampering," or "eliminating" they seem to be at the center of it. This makes no surprise to see the basic foundation of what we know of as history was made by a key Jesuit scholar.

For me however I find Scaliger interesting, first of all for the fact that the Jesuit leaders of the Vatican were rather upset with his interpretations of history. I wonder if there had been much more in Scaliger's original work that might have over time been carefully "edited" out. But what remains is actually very interesting. Unlike the rest of the revision community, I am very much on the fence with him because prior to his writing most ancient history was only thought of as the Romans and Greeks It was Scaliger who brought Ancient Egypt, Persia, and Babylon into their own. Granted he worked within the earth is only 6000 years old thesis (standard belief structure of all Christian scholarship of the day), and all of his history had to fit in that timeframe. Scaliger worked certainly with revising history, but I would more concerned about Petavius and other later historians, who completed Scaliger's work to please Jesuit leaders.

Fomenko claims that most all history was fabricated by the Vatican, the Holy Roman Empire and the pro-German Romanov dynasty (three main enemies historical of Russia). His theories attempt to put Russia at the center of ancient civilization, by proposing a giant "Russian Horde" empire and eliminating historical time before its existence. A second major belief of his is that a great ancient civilization once existed in the area where Russia today is, called the great Tartary. It can be found on many ancient maps of the time, and likely was erased by historical accounts. In fact Fomenko claims that this "kingdom" stretched as far as what is known as the American West. That the cities such as Chicago, San Francisco or Salt Lake City were part of this Tartarian empire.

Unfortunately now this word, Tartaria, has become a catch all word to mean anything from an unknown civilization in our not so remote past. Some believe that this seemingly similar world wide civilization were all Russians, others (myself included) believe that the sections of the world were a connected series of empires. There might have been a Tartaria, and a Rome, and an America. But now the researchers of the day use the name Tartaria for everywhere in the world the see beautiful old architecture. Was Russia likely a key part of this worldwide ancient civilization? Most definitely. But within this last 1 to 2,000 years I don't see indications that one of these areas are more important than another. Like separate departments of a big company, each had its area, role, expertise- but they were always part of the one large company, linked by the common mythology, architecture, religion, connection to nature, and understanding of reality.[84]

"Even though the writings have been interpreted by Egyptologists, they have little understanding of the thoughts and beliefs expressed in them, as modern English teachers have little understanding of the Hermetic philosophy enshrined in Shakespeare." John Anthony West, Serpent vii

But then we come to reason that that I disagree with Fomenko. That is his belief that what we call the Ancient Rome, Ancient Greece and Ancient Egypt etc. actually occurred during the Middle Ages (1000-1500AD our current timeline), and as suggested some even go so far as to believe that French soldiers built the Egyptian pyramids in the 1800's. My research has been to change the historical timelines of Egypt, Mexico, and Peru...but not to move it closer to our period, but much farther back in history- greater even than 10,000 years.

It is this part of his theory that most concerns me, because it creates a questioning of his research. It has been the historical trend for the last 500 years to try and take away what the most special of ancient of sites are- structures unique to this planet, something that can not be

---

[84] Fomenko claims that the most probable prototype of the historical Jesus was Andronikos I Komnenos (allegedly AD 1152 to 1185), the emperor of Byzantium. He seems to not focus enough on why the Jesus story is basically exactly the same story as

Bacchus, Dionysius, Krishna, Osiris and others. There is one root for this, and I am hoping to have a new book out in a year or so that helps explain where the original Jesus story originates.

built today, even with modern machines. The largest pyramids, beyond the massive blocks and perfect masonry, are infused with layer upon layer of geometry, mathematics, and vibrational fields. Christopher Dunn may be the closest when he called them ancient power plants. How exactly French soldiers, or even people at the time Ancient Rome could build these giants at Daschur and Giza is never explained? Or how granite blocks have holes and cuts in them that show signs of laser tools and diamond tipped drills. The archaeological story of copper tools and slaves pulling stones is beyond disappointing. Something far more advanced had to be used- but as long as the copper tool and ramps are presented by the "experts" the average person won't think anything about it. Pyramid sites, and other world sites like Pumu Punku are very special places, places that can actually take humans to another level if they were allowed to fully access the energy available. That is why those in control of this place want to keep people from accessing the inherent power of these sites.

Archaeologists try to stop people from thinking about the ancient world, and it seems Fomenko's chronology does the same thing. Fomenko focuses almost nothing on the great places of Egypt, such as the Oserion at Abydos or Teotihucan in Mexico. Instead he focus on some Egyptian horoscopes from Dendera and Esna (Greek period temples) and claim to date them to 1000 AD. If anyone should be absolutely shocked by the brilliance of place like Giza Pyramids it should be a mathematician. But Fomenko is not impressed by the perfect geometry, or astronomy that has been encoded in the monuments. And that makes me wonder.

The only way you can know an ancient site is to study it personally, not through a book, but by being there. Fomenko it seems did not do that. What books (or internet investigation) can do provide background and familiarity with a site to prepare you for the visit. The books are a preparation for, not a replacement, for the in person- on site examination and investigation. Only by "feeling" a site can you get to know it. How it energized (or in some cases weakens) the energy structure is just as important as what it was built with, how and when. I don't want to go further into this, only to mention it to you to keep in mind as you contemplate the very ancient past. But, this book is looking more at the last few hundred years, so let us move on in our presentation of terms.

*

CATHEDRALS and STAR FORTS

Chartres Cathedral

The word antique-tech being thrown around for what seems to be a lost type of technology in our recent past. Generally it refers to things such as towers and domes of cathedrals, or star forts, but can also refer various applications from fireplaces to early transport. The place to start the examination of the word's reference is with Medieval Cathedrals.

I now believe that Cathedrals originally had nothing to do with religion, in fact what we call Christianity might be a very recent invention. When this new religion (or what might be called a new form of a very old religion) took over, they merely converted the existing specific designed buildings in all cities into modern churches. The Pantheon in Rome is a good example of a building with originally one purpose being taken over to become a church.

I think all of the pre 1800 churches were the great energy centers of their day. When pyramids could no longer be built 4000 years ago, the switch was made to large temple structures (such as Luxor and Karnak). This perhaps lasted one or two thousand years when another

177

change came. During the next phase of building came what we now cal Cathedrals. A major feature is their giant towers and domes, used tc bring down the energy of the atmosphere. To help this feature, the roofs of the towers or domes include some form of copper and often balls of liquid mercury. Sometimes the mercury was placed within vases or statues that line the roof. Take a look under the dome of the German Reichstag, and one will find a very odd gigantic copper coil, pointing down from the dome. It really make no sense from the standpoint of ornamentation, but if the dome is instead actually a type of electrica energy generator, then it makes much more sense as to why such a copper coil would be present. I believe is we were allowed a detailed examination of the world's great cathedrals we will find similar things.

Rose window, St Nicholas Cathedral, Nantes

Also the buildings were constructed on top of an energy spot or the earth (often on top an older structure from the temple building period), in order to combine the energy from the ground with the sky. This energy could then either be used by the building in question, or amplified and sent out to the entire city. The stone and its layout make the building a giant machine, which spirals the energy drawn from the sky and earth within the cathedral. It will then, perhaps after the addition of organ music, be sent out of through the giant rose windows (which are made in the shape of cymatic wave patterns) into the city now charged with that particular frequency. Each rose window is in fact a frequency projection device based on the geometric pattern on which it was formed. Added to this is the phenomenal carving that these cathedrals have (both inside and outside) either in the form of

178

decorative shapes or statues. While adding to the overall beauty, they are also there to act as energy resonators and amplifiers. Thus you must think of cathedrals as vibrational generators, similar to a temple such as Karnak or Luxor, where every stone, relief and carving is all a prat of the created vibrational energy makeup. There was a reason Pythagoras and Goethe both claimed that architecture was "music frozen in stone."

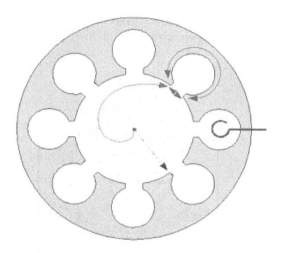

Magnetron, looking very similar to rose windows and even *The Pantheon in Rome.*

To add a bit of modern science to the discussion, I present three terms- magnetron, cathode and resonance. A cavity magnetron "is a high-powered vacuum tube that generates microwaves using the interaction of a stream of electrons with a magnetic field while moving past a series of open metal cavities (cavity resonators). Electrons pass by the cavities and cause radio waves to oscillate within, similar to the way a whistle produces a tone when excited by an air stream blown past its opening."[85] So what does that mean? It means that the way the device is constructed will create and amplify a microwave frequency.

An early form of the magnetron was invented in 1910, and another by General Electric in 1920, but it was not until the 1940's when German, Russian and British researchers used these ideas to improve radar technology. The magnetron works with resonance, and any device that shows such properties is known as a resonator. Musical instruments

---

[85] Wikipedia magnetron

179

use acoustic resonators that produce sound waves of specific tones while quartz crystals (used in electronic devices such as radio transmitters and quartz watches) will produce oscillations of very precise frequency. Some musical instruments generate the sound directly, such as the wooden bars in a xylophone, the head of a drum, the strings in stringed instruments, or the pipes in an organ. Some modify the sound by enhancing particular frequencies, such as the sound box of a guitar or violin. Many five-string banjos have removable resonators, so players can use the instrument with a resonator in bluegrass style, or without it in folk music style.

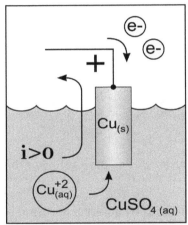

Diagram of a copper cathode

Very interesting is the cathode, which is a word very close to the word cathedral. A cathode was named by Michael Faraday in the 1830's and comes from the Greek word for "descent," which is what the energy in one is doing. Perhaps the buildings were really called cath-odrals at one time, or perhaps it was in these buildings were Faraday got his inspiration? It is very hard to explain what a cathode is, sort of like a battery, but it does mimic much of what the cathedrals are in fact doing. Recall that many cathodes use copper as their main actor, as in the diagram above. This would explain the need for cathedrals to have copper on their roofs. What is amazing is that this technology has been around us for hundreds of years, and no one has noticed until just recently.[86] Another scientific term is the fractal tower, which uses a type of repeated triangle or square over and over to increase the amount of waves the antenna can receive, while lessening its surface area. Many of the towers on top of cathedrals, castles or palaces have this fractal appearance, as to all of the world's star forts.

So what happened with all this energy being generated? On one hand I think the energy is still being generated by the cathedrals. I have traveled around Europe checking great cathedrals I come across, from Chartres to the Duomo in Florence, to various cathedrals from Rome to Nantes. Generally, not always there are a few exceptions, but the level of energy that I notice within the cathedral is staggering. In fact it seems like the large columns, that run down either side of the nave are a part of the energy function to move what comes from the domes and towers to ground level. There are passages along either side, and I can at time feel the energy moving down these passageway as if the energy is in fact circling around. The pipe organs are not there for show, or add nice music to a sermon. They were part of the original technology of the cathedral device. By adding an extra element of specific musical vibration at very high dosses, I think could allow the generated energy to be projected out of the rose windows. Tesla tower technology is basically what these cathedrals are doing.

At times I still think that energy does go out, but except for those living close by, the energy will be dissipated as nothing outside of the building is collecting it now. A receiver of some type is needed to harness it. At one time I believe the places people lived were set up in such a way to harness and use this energy being projected from the cathedrals. For example, in Nantes I noticed (and then remembered in many other European cities I had visited) that most of the apartments all had all iron bars in front of their windows. I do not think that it accident. I think the iron was the conductor for the energy coming from the churches. I think the energy was attracted to the iron, and then within each home was another device (that might not even have been recognized as a device but a simple household tool) that could bring the energy from the iron gates inside, where anything needed to be powered had a source of energy. So great might this have been that these buildings (And why there are so many in cities) was to provide enough harmonious energy to keep all of the city healthy and happy. In fact hospitals may to have been needed, just go into the cathedral for a while to be re harmonized.

---

[86] I recommended the youtube video Free Energy Magnetron by jonlevi, and the original video on the subject by globalvision

I also want to point out that old ornate fireplaces that were found in palaces and in early homes. What is most fascinating about them, more than their amazing intricate design work, was that the were unable to have wood burned in them, and they were far too big to keep any heat in the giant rooms even if wood could be burned. Some in fact had no chimney. So these could not be fireplaces as we have been led to believe, but some type of technology- where in a palace (often far away from cathedrals but which had towers and dome on top of the palace) generated the energy itself that somehow transferred to these giant iron hotboxes. In some way they would heat up in winter without the need for wood or coal. Thus creating perfectly "clean green" energy heating. It seems that paired ornaments on the front of them, perhaps made of iron or copper, acted like an energy drawing device (similar to obelisks in front of Egyptian temples). This great technology was lost after the "reset" of the 1800's, and the fireplaces had to be converted to burn wood and coal.

There seems to have been utility poles way back in the 1860's. Old Russian photographs are good to show these. There are no wires attached to any of them, so they are not early telephone or telegraph wires. The suggestion is this energy transferred form the entry point (cathedral or other dome tower building) to these poles, where each home or business could tap into the source. All wireless transmission, and all free.

Town of Palmanova, Italy.

The world is covered with star forts. Claimed to simply be easy for defense (many canons to fire off the same line) there is something odd that I never noticed about them. The first is their intricate geometric design patters (similar in many cases to the beauty of the rose windows of Cathedrals or snowflakes), the water that surrounds them, and the stories throughout history of armies not able to conquer them, no matter the weaponry at hand (Prince of Wales Star Fort in Northern Manitoba is such an example).

The research now seems to indicate that there were defensive protection, but not how one thinks. Most early European cities were surrounded by such star fortress protection (now mostly dismantles for expansive city building). Something about the shape not only created a harmonic energy pattern within the area of the walls, but also were able to protect the city (or space) from energy or sound related attacks. Bible stories such as a trumpet being used to knock down the walls of Jericho are not simple metaphor. Sound has great power, and harnessed as a weapon is near impossible to stop. Cathedrals and star forts, along with their other purposes may have helped to protect cities from sound based attacks- at least for a long while, for as the chapter on Fires seems to indicate, something was eventually able to penetrate their defenses. The star forts are laid out as a world wide grid, and they may interact with each other. Thus the more star forts that were "active" and being used might have in a sense made each in the series stronger-operating almost like a giant set of interconnected batteries.

*

ART

      I want to present why this ancient architecture is important from the standpoint of energy and psychology. When see any moderr building (such as the New Chicago Federal Building of he 1960's ir chapter 3), all it is functional use of space. It is in fact devoid of soul, devoid of energy because it is not built from ancient principles. That symbolizes our modern world. Now look again at the building from 1908. It has energy, and life, and more. It is almost alive, bringing Greece, Rome and Egypt to our doorsteps and lives. And that is because I dc not think these "older" buildings are emulating a style from the Ancient World, they may have been part of that same World. The builders of the modern fairs were far closer in time to the Parthenon in Greece than the later modern building. Not only have we been lied to, we have had the very structures that create harmony, healing, and balance taken away. They were not just things to look nice (though great effort was done to do just that) their entire layout, geometry, use of Tesla energy, sound cymatics and the like went into them. It might have become a courthouse after the "reset" of the 1850's...but what it was before that is unknown. Perhaps part of a giant whole of harmonic principles equal to what can be found in Chartres, The Duomo, Luxor Temple or any great edifice. These truly are/were temples, and we are losing the few that are left daily. How soon might all the memory of these buildings be gone, lost in the tenor that modern art (a few black lines drawn on canvas, or the new Federal Building).

      I never understood why this was true until I ran into the book Serpent in the Sky by John Anthony West, who used an entire chapter to present how ancient viewed art. Which was not something to be looked at, or create certain feelings or ideas in the person looking at it- but to create universal harmony. The same principle in every single person viewing it should occur from the art, in fact the very space on earth- to harmonize sky and ground and person and animal in one infused harmonic whole. It can been seen in every statue or painting in Florence, every cathedral, every monastery. That was the old world...the world the modern has wanted to destroy to control the minds of the masses...and make all of us unquestioning slaves.

How the lines on a canvas can possibly compare to Da Vinci's Annunciation, or Botticelli's Primavera is beyond me. It again shows just how many levels of brainwashing has occurred. Do not forget, that one of the main financiers of Modern Art Museums was John Rockefeller. He was not putting his money into something to help humanity, but help his elite cause. Brainwash the people into thinking the old beauty needs to be destroyed or hidden in the back of a museum, while the new modern soul-less junk is portrayed as the ideal.

Annunciation by Da Vinci, Uffizi Gallery Florence

I saw this displayed again just recently on a research trip to Nantes, France (a former ancient White City). The main level of the art gallery is stunning. Beautiful ancient building, with beautiful 16 and 17 th century religious and wisdom style art. So perfect it appears as if the paintings are photographs. Layered with symbolism and perfected geometry. But then my wife and I decided to take a quick look at the modern art section before we left. While of course ugly, when we reached what was called the chapel we got the shock of shocks. Here a beautiful 1700's church had most of the artwork and fine sculpture removed (though bits of it were still left higher on the walls). What would have been an ornate ceiling was layered over with a series of wooden planks. Inside were 40 television sets, all blaring children or older people screaming or blowing whistles or cars exploding. This is what

185

was being presented as art, while the very building used to present it-actual ancient art of soul and harmony was mostly destroyed to showcase the modern lie. Nothing presented this loss and this brainwashing of the masses more clearly than this. Go to Nantes to see it, but start at the chapel to get it out of your system. Finish your experience with two hours of the beauty. That is where the power and healing is. That is what our world should, and used, to be.

*

MUDFLOOD

This is now a catch all word to describe what seem to be a period of recent cataclysms, mostly focused on the 1800's (especially the periods around 1812 and 1850) but might go back to the 15 or 1600's. Many take the term literally, referring to giant floods that left cities buried in mud. This can be deduced from old photographs of buildings literally sunk down in mud- and from many buildings from the period that still exist today that seem to have their lower stories partway underground (which is not how you would build), or doors that require many stairs up to reach when just below is what appears to be a similar door but now far below street level. There are thousands of photos on the internet, and I suggest if this is a new term for you to go and take a look at some of them. They truly are fascinating where it appears that almost every city in the 1800's had mounds of mud all around mud only streets- yet have phenomenal architecture all around. It makes you wonder that if you were going to build giant cathedrals and buildings with marble and other stone, would you also not take the ti me to make a proper street to make getting the materials to it much easier? But here in the 1800's they were left with mud streets, and cities of spectacular buildings.

Yet what the word really is pointing to is a period of disaster and chaos that came to the cites of the world during this time period. These may have been floods (of mud or water), earthquakes, volcanoes, fires, warfare, EMF weapons, germ warfare or whatnot. What does seem to be is that the period was recent (200 or so years ago) and world wide, which decimated both the cities and the population within them. This period seems to be connected to large periods of wars. Perhaps the wars were wars, or they may have been semi-staged events to explain the destruction and emptying of cities, while using soldiers to round up survivors. Such events as the Napoleonic Wars or the American Civil War are up for question as to the true happenings of them. But it seems hundreds of millions of people died off during this period of time, the questions are how and why.

Almost every major city in the early stages of photography (1860-80) seem to be photographed totally in tact, or in semi ruins- but there are no people on the streets. Be it St Petersburg, San Francisco, Paris, they are devoid of people, horses, carts, in fact life. And when people do appear they tend to be groups of children with no adults to be found anywhere. All of this again is very strange and no sufficient answer for it has yet been provided.

*

RESET

In the alternate historical context, this word refers to something similar as it does in computer terminology. When your computer freezes, or the game you are playing is no longer interesting, you do a reset and start over from the beginning. This theory claims that a group of beings control the actions of this planet. Generally this controlling group is labeled by such terms as Illuminati or Freemasons. This force has only one thing in mind, its own benefit and survival. They are basically a parasitic force, and we are its main food source.[87]

When things seem to go too far (humans know too much of what is going on)- the system is shut down and re populated (many speculations of how that is done). The surviving group is quickly made ignorant of the past, and become slaves for the in-between elite. This can link to the strange orphan trains (seemingly thousands of children being sent on trains to Western US cities, though there is no real good answer as to where all these children came from) or why all of a sudden in the 1800's was a need for massive orphanages. It is like some sort of virus came and wiped out all the adult population leaving only tens of thousands of children alive. A population of just children would be rather easy to brainwash into believing any story of the past you wanted. The other thing that rises at this time are insane asylums. Hundreds of them, all in what we today would call giant palaces. First why the need for so many, and why must they all rival Buckingham Palace for their size and ornateness?

---

[87] Castaneda and many writers were clear that what we think of as our mind is parasitic invasion from an outside source.

187

I think they were not the original function, but old buildings that were confiscated for a new purpose. The insane asylums were for anyone who was not agreeing with the new "story" being presented for history. If you remembered the old magnificence of the buildings and who really lived there and how to use the energy, you were put in the insane asylum and tortured until you were fully brainwashed and forgot the past (so could be sent out) or just killed off so as no one could hear your old memories. The same thing basically happened to the taken over Native Indians, who were sent to reservations to be hidden away from the rest of society, and children sent to schools where they were tortured into forgetting everything about their culture. If you would not go along with the story you were deemed crazy and sent to a mental hospital for "reindoctrination" which is why so many asylums all of a sudden turn up at this time

What we call natives, might either be groups on the periphery of the old ancient civilization (a sort of land-nature direct caretaker for the main cities) or could in fact be the old civilization who survived the attacks, were driven out of their cities to survive as long as they could in the wilds. I also feel that stories such as the Cathars and Knights Templar and others are not separate events- but all a part of the same destruction of humanity in the last reset- and may have all taken place much later than currently presented, even as late as between 1650-1812.

Lastly as mentioned, who so many photos of cities that are in perfect condition, with no construction of any kind happening- yet are missing one thing. Life of any kind. No people, no horses, no garbage flying around, no smoke from chimneys. Nothing to indicate life, like it is a photo of computer generated city we see in architectural plans. The standard claim for the lack of life was the long processing speed photography needed at this time or would create blurring. Ok, so where is the blurring? Or did they manage to send away the 250,000 people and horses, and dogs and cats out of St Petersburg for the day so they could take photos? And the same with photos of Toronto, Boston, Paris, Helsinki, Rome, or San Francisco from this time- all resulting in a complete very "lifeless" city similar to Chinese cities today that have been built but have no people living in them.

I see several of these resets happening over history. One was at the end of the pyramid building period. Another may have happened at the end of the temple building period, and another more recent one at the end of what might be called the post Greco-Roman period. This theory leads far more credence to what we call "life on earth" more being some type of an experiment, or computer simulation- controlled by basic coding (laws of nature) that can get bent by the outside forces to control the game or experiment as they wish. It seems we too have some ability to hack into the same mainframe as the "controllers" and alter things along the way- and people like the great alchemists, Pythagoras or ancient masters each had learned their own way to "hack into the mainframe" of reality and make changes as needed.

Some suggest another reset is coming, but I am not so sure. If they happen when humans have too much control and power, and our world today is showcased by how little control and power the average human has. Or maybe humans are much closer to opening a giant doorway of understanding worldwide and a reset would be required to happened before that occurs. This is semi speculation of course, time will tell, and more importantly this chapter is about preparing you for the meaning of the words being used now in the research around these topics.

*

PHOTOGRAPHY

Standard history claims photography, as we know it, was not invented until around 1800, the oldest surviving images are from 1826, and by 1840 photography has moved into decent quality. That is a very fast movement for the technology. And the invention seems to have be just in time to produce images at the very period where history seems like it was getting overturned, rewritten, and completely changed.

But what if photography has a different history? What if it is much older? There were devices known as Camera Obscura during the Renaissance. Da Vinci is claimed to have either had one or at least drawn the plans for one. That many drawings of the pre photography era are incredibly detailed, might indicate that the artist was working with some type of early photograph and did a partial tracing over it to get the drawn image so correct. We have many instances of seeing this even since 1850, where a drawing or postcard has been made, and then the photograph it was taken from can be found. Here is an example,

189

Postcard SF Exposition 1915

Original Photograph, SF Exposition 1915

So here are two examples from the San Francisco Exposition. The postcard is an obvious drawing of the photograph, just with the woman in the front right of the photo removed. So we have to question all the drawings we have. We can find similar drawing copies from the 1800's that are from real photographs. Look back to the drawing of the supposed raising of Chicago in 1858 in chapter 3. We have the drawing,

190

but we also for this one have the original photograph that the drawing was modeled on. We can see that the drawing has been greatly "dramatized" in fact even made inaccurate from the photo to try and present the "story" rather than fact. How many more photos from the past really exist?

How far back does photography go? Some now suggest it might go back at least to the Greek age in some form, for Plato could not have written his allegory of the Cave without understanding of what we call modern camera and motion projectors. If photography is much older than believed, and if you have access to a photograph from say 1700, it can be easy to take it and clam it to be from 1870- because no one would believe there could be photo from before the 1850. Just because we have an old photo, and that it presented and dated to a certain year, we know only that we have an image. We can not really be sure of the date that image was actually taken, only the date currently presented to us- which may or may not be correct.

So back to the early photographs of ornate buildings with little around them. Perhaps the photos are hundreds of years older than claimed? Could the Vatican and Smithsonian not just be hiding all the great books and manuscripts of the past, might they also be storing all of the early photographs? If an ancient people had the technology to build these massive buildings- would they also not have had photographic equipment also? The photos were preserved, just like we do, then later used by the new controller to present ancient buildings as modern by revealing a "building" photo. No one would question that it was not from 1854, because no one was supposed to have cameras before that. No one, even today could even ponder that perhaps the photo is from 1854, or 1754 or 1254. I always find it odd how often the date was placed on old photographs, as if the need to date the photograph at the time was very very important.

*

CITY FIRES AND DISASTERS

Baltimore 1904

I have mentioned many times that it seems every city in North America had a great fire between 1800-1910. Ok not seems, they did. Toronto, Boston, Philadelphia, Portland, Ottawa, Jacksonville, Seattle, Calgary, Vancouver, Baltimore. To copy the complete list from wikipedia would take the better part of two whole pages of this book. It is so co-incidental as to not be a co-incidence. Then following the fires, the cities go through "magical rebuilds," at a scale that is basically impossible. Something is very odd about these fires. So great is this topic that it demands an entire book of itself. I will only provide a brief overview. I am hoping that a site like stolenhistory.org, will take their online research and put it into a book.

*

I wanted to start again with the Chicago Fire of October 8, 1871. The fire who for over one hundred years was claimed to have begun when a wayward cow knocked over a candle.

Chicago fire 1871

The first thing to realize is that this fire was not in isolation. There were four giant fires that very day all along Lake Michigan- in Peshtigo, Wisconsin (where 2,500 people died), Holland Michigan, and Manistee Michigan. Four great fires on the same day in the same general location is too co-incidental. Ignatius Donnely, author and scientist, suggested in the 1880's that the fires must have been caused my a meteor strike. In 2004 physicist Robert Wood named it as Bela's Comet specifically. The story that a running cow could have started this blaze in Chicago, is a nice story for kids to believe (like the easter bunny or santa claus) so as to not have anyone do real thinking about it. Yet anyone close to Chicago at the time would have seen through the "cow" story right away- especially with three other serious fires close by. At the Peshtigo fire a local priest was quoted as suggesting that "things came from the sky causing the fires," which could mean meteors...but even could mean many things. All he said was things coming from the sky. Because what is for sure that when looking at the photos above, we are not seeing fires. And the same becomes true when we look at the photos of the other city fires. And when we look at artwork of the 15-1600's that depict balls of light falling into burning cities, balls that could even look like modern missiles. So what happened?

193

One the building contractors I met has seen fire damage to buildings many times. He was very clear when looking at the fire photos of Chicago and several other cities that they were not fires. In fact he asked, "who bombed this city, because this damage is not from a fire. Look all these buildings were stone, not wood, and the stone is flaking off. That is serious damage. A simple fire can not do this to stone. Take the cathedral in Paris that just burned...ya Notre Dame. The ceiling burned because it was made of wood. But the stone structure of the building turned out fine, a bit of soot damage to change the colour but that's it. Now look at these photos. What has done this to the stone? This really needs to be examined farther."

Go and look at more photos. They can be found all over the internet. Try Portland Maine 1866, Boston 1872 or Toronto 1904. The fires were claimed to have been so bad because all of the buildings were built of wood. But when you look at the photos carefully all I can see is brick and stone. And pulverized brick and stone at that. Again no char marks, no sign of fire- just "battle damaged" stone buildings.

Portland, Maine 1866

I could post photo after photo, from city after city, and they would look very similar. Again look at all the brick and stone surviving, and how much of it has in a sense been turned to powder. Stone in many cases has been melted, or sliced in half and what not.[88] Meanwhile trees, electrical poles and even vegetation remain completely in tact.

Boston fire 1872

We have two more oddities with the presentation of the city fires. The first is that though they cause tremendous damage, very few people died (often just one or two). Would not many more be swept by it at night, caught in the upper floors of buildings? Maybe the few death results are a message. We also have the odd photos of people posing for "selfies" with the destruction in the background (such as in San Francisco) or with many military troops standing in front of the fire damage, almost as if they are showing off a trophy.

Another is all the Civil War photographs of cities destroyed in the Southern US. Look carefully at Richmond Virginia or other cities. First what you see are remnants of spectacular Roman and Greek style buildings. Then what you see from destruction is not really what would be capable of cannon attacks of that time. Unless you took 50 cannons, stood them outside of buildings and fired over and over again for hours. It is more like controlled dynamite to the buildings, or some other form of high powered attack. That possibly means the Civil War could be nothing like we have been told, that it may have not been a real war, but a mop up operation to destroy architecture in Southern US States, and round up remaining "survivors." That is how screwed up what we call

---

[88] Interestingly the same strange heat damage, can be found in some temples in Egypt such as Tanis and Abu Sir where granite statues and temples show signs of having been melted from super high heat, and could indicate that such "disasters" did not just happen in the 1800's but have been a long part of the real history of earth.

195

standard history might be, even wars were not really wars anything like we have been told.

Some in this alternative historical research community believe that these fires might be plasma discharges from the solar system (or dome firmament depending who is making the suggestion). Others see them as deliberately started (perhaps EMP devices), in order to destroy many of the old ancient buildings of the cities. Or at least as a way to kill off the inhabitants very quickly without the need for ground warfare. It is definitely something to think of, for there is almost no US or Canadian city in the late 1800's early 1900's that did not go through a major fire.

Which tends to lead me that those fires, and possibly the ones from the 1800's, are a form of microwave attack. Because if you put aluminum or metal into a microwave and turn it on, it will quickly catch fire. But have some broccoli or a carrot next to it, and nothing will happen to them, other then they get a bit wilted and soggy. This type of thing was clear to see in the California wildfires, and I see the same in all the aftermath photos of the 1800's fires.

So what happened here? Was it a fire as said? Some sort of bombing attack? A EMP or microwave attack that could target buildings and people, even target specific buildings and areas? A few even claim that it is the result of an HG Wells real life War of the Worlds alien attack and takeover of earth. I am not going to go that far, but again since we have no idea what really occurred here, even that has to be kept on the table as possibility. Recall Wells wrote that story in the 1890's in England, almost at the end of this fire phenomena.

Do I believe that the photos we see of the destruction are genuine. Very much so. But I speculate that the photos are perhaps not in the year claimed, but perhaps hundreds of years previous. Perhaps 1771 for Chicago and 1789 for Seattle for example. That then allows for an extra 100 years to rebuild the destroyed city which would make more sense from standard building logic. But this is not believed because photography was not supposed to be invented until the 1830's. That would mean that high quality photography has been along a lot longer than history claims. That is something to keep in mind. We really do not know just how old photography really is, but only trust the history of it- of an object supposedly created during the very time frame in question- when real history of the period was being covered up and lied about. On the other hand we have newspaper reports about the fires, usually coming out the next day, and offering "official narrative reasons" for the fire. Cow knocks over a bucket, girl is playing with matches, bird knocks over some glue or some other goofy story. Never again examined or looked at.

I may also speculate that the fires/disasters are not years apart, happening in every city in North American over a 100 year period. My guess they might be one continent wide event. Less if it is was some sort of continent wide natural disaster such as earthquakes, volcanoes, or even actual attacks by unknown technology on every city in North America. To present all the "fires" in their correct years would lead to obvious questions. So they spread out the dates to make it look like just random acts. While I can not fully prove it yet, the hunches and circumstantial evidence are pointing to the fire being in some form an "act of war."

While at this point I, nor it seems does anyone else, have the answers as to what really happened in our recent past. All we can tell at this point is that our past, heritage, knowledge, health and life were all taken from us. All with this knowledge were gotten rid of: be they Indians, Cathars, Romans, Ancient Egyptians, Americans, Tartarians, you name it. The Native Indians, Cathars and the population of Ancient Rome might all have been getting slaughtered at the same moment, just at different places on the earth.

I have often hated to read books that pose a number of very interesting problems and questions, but then seem never to offer much in the way of answers to those issues at the end. Documentaries are famous for this. Granted they hook the reader-viewer at the beginning by promising to "answer the unsolved question of" (whatever the subject is from pyramids to Custer to Stalingrad). Yet nothing is answered. The difference here, I hope, is that I did not start at the beginning of this book by saying I had answers. What I did have was enough evidence to present that standard history of the most recent 200 years of our timeline is a giant lie. I of course did not get into such recent such as the JFK assassination, the moon landings, exploration of Antarctica, and other recent obvious lies. But what needs to be understood, is that all of those recent lies all come out of the period 1776-1945. That period of time is the foundation of everything that has come after.

I am hopeful more deeper answers will appear as this research investigation into the historical lies of our recent past continues. Of course truth eventually will be revealed, but it might take a long time for that to occur.

I am just touching this subject briefly, but I do feel that it needs far more attention and study. A few good researchers should get together to write a detailed book on this odd city destruction phenomena of the 1800's. Why not me you ask? Well I have other projects now to focus on, and while this one does interest me and I will follow along if research continues to uncover interesting information- as I say, I have to move to other areas.

It is going to be a ride for everyone who devotes time to this study...my best wishes to everyone in their research into the truth of our past.

CHAPTER 8
ANCIENT ROME-
The Missing Link

Remains of Temple of Antonius and Fostina in the Roman Forum

I wondered for a while if these Expositions may have been modeled on something specific. Just flipping channels I came across a documentary presenting a site in Ancient Rome that just recently opened to the public. As I looked at the TV screen as they displayed a computer generated reconstruction of what Nero's Domus Aurea (Golden House) would have looked like, I almost shouted at the screen, "look it's the Chicago Exposition, or St. Louis. That's it. This is the missing piece." This will be a short chapter, but that does not mean that it is not important in our understanding of the 1800's. I want you to see how many of the features that I will be listing are the same as the fairs. I can now safely say that it is highly likely that the big US Exhibitions of the late 19 th century were not only in some way "copying" Ancient Rome- they were specifically copying the Domus Aurea. The question is only when the copy was being built.

The Domus Aurea in Rome *"has been considered a landmark in the history of Roman architecture, often cited as an example of innovative construction, sophistication and spatial planning- and deliberate, if not ostentatious decoration."*[89] Claimed by historians to

---

[89]The Domus Aurea Reconsidered, by P Gregory Warden

have been built by Nero in 64 AD, following the destruction of much of downtown Rome from a great fire (That is the same story as would be Chicago, San Francisco and the other exposition cities. Was there really a fire and earthquake, or was one "needed" in order to keep with the symbolism of the Domus Aurea). Nero was one of the first line of new Roman emperors, coming up as a teenager, and this was claimed for his need to have to build on a large scale to show off his power to his rivals. That is how modern historians think, but perhaps Nero was doing something completely different, and this new giant area was to be his way of starting a new Rome.

Remains of the massive Domus Aurea, without its marble walls and fantastic frescoes in most cases, this is what one tends to see mostly when touring it.

It became the biggest palace in all of Rome, built beside the Palantine Hill and across from the Forum. It was a massive area of 200 acres with a giant lake, parkland, gardens, pastures and a vineyard. The countryside was recreated in the middle of Rome. Of course there were massive buildings, with domes, and columns. The interior was made of brick (as shown above), with solid concrete and marble on the outside on the outside. The style and size of structures certainly kept with the premise of the look of Rome being a "Great White City," the nickname given for the Chicago Exhibition. Yet it had the name the Golden Palace, for it shone, either due to gold covering, pearls and jewels or perhaps electric power. The palace was put up in the record time of just four years (as the modern fairs are claimed to all be built in record time) by the two architects Celer and Severu. Pliny the Elder mentions he watched its construction in his book *Naturalis Historia*. When completed Sevtonius claimed Nero responded that "he had at last begun to live like a human being."

Author photo of a reconstruction of the Domus Aurea projected onto the wall at the start of the underground tour. Domus Aura or 1890's Exposition? That could easily be the Great Basin of the Columbian Exposition.

Nero wanted music, statues, painting, poetry to be presented and displayed. One of the centerpieces was a giant 35.5 m high bronze statue, the Colossus Neronis. The statue could be found outside of the entrance. Inside the rooms were spectacular, all made with polished marble, with extra windows and niches to let in more light, while pools and fountains were in the rooms (to provide sound as well as keep the air cool in summer months). The ceilings were covered with mosaic tiles in the ceilings, and the most lavish paintings were on the walls. It is claimed that it is these wall paintings that inspired the paintings of the mid-Renaissance artists such as Raphael's Vatican Stanze and 18th-century Neoclassicism.

201

The central oculus of the octagonal court of the Domus Aurea.

One of the great features was a fantastic octagonal court. The dome, one of the most amazing of its day in concrete, had a central oculus to let in light. The Pantheon in miniature. A giant fountain ran at one end underneath the floor, offering not only to regulate temperature but also to act in the same way as water beneath the pyramids might operate (as an energy conducting device). Energetically the room is spectacular...and it needs to be imagined with the marble walls and floors, fantastic statues

Statue said to have been in the Domus Aurea, now in the Vatican Museum.

There are a lot of problems with the presentation of this as a palace. The first is that it is claimed that there were no kitchens or bathrooms.[90] No kitchens or bathrooms, so who is supposed to be living there? I enjoyed another documentary on this place, as they depicted lavish Roman feasts, with everyone eating and drinking to excess...but umm, there are no kitchens. So just where was all this food coming from? Where would they go to the bathroom? Certainly not in the giant lake in the center of the palace. It links to similar structures of the early modern time where we see palaces with giant fireplaces (with no way of burning wood in them), and massive hotels without bathrooms. Did people actually need to eat? Don't gloss over that too quickly. Could they have been obtaining their energy requirements from the air, the sun, or the buildings themselves? We are now speculating that the old fireplaces were linked to the towers on the palace roofs that seemed to bring energy into the space to heat without the need of any burning wood or coal. The ancient fireplaces are in fact a form of sophisticated technology. Moreso, at the Domus Aurea there have been found no places for anyone to sleep. So it is not a hotel, or a residence. It was a place only to visit. Does this sound like the Exhibitions of the 19 th century?

---

[90] https://www.rome-museum.com/domus-aurea.php

Incredible bathtub of Nero claimed to be in the Domus Area, now on a beautiful mosaic floor in an octagonal room in the Vatican Museum. Like others, the diorite has been smoothed to an almost glass-like surface.

Even more amazing was another court that rotated. Yes rotated! Some historians claim it was just the dome the did the rotating, while others claim it was the entire structure. Most historians present that it was made to move by slaves cranking a series of revolving mechanisms, but that is only speculation. To date no one has any idea how the revolving was done, how much of it revolved, or what the reason was for it. Just that they had one.

The Flavian Amphitheater (Coliseum) was built overtop of the great lake of the Domus Aurea.

Nero then died in 68AD, and so too it seems his "palace." Soon after his death the entire area was filled in, and the Trajan's Baths and a Temple of Venus built over top of it in 79 AD. That means according to the standard history this giant complex was only used for 4 years by Nero, then completely covered over ten years later. On top of the lake was built the Flavian Amphitheater. Yes, they built the Coliseum on top of the lake. Remember of the claims that the Coliseum twice a week had the entire floor flooded to stage mock naval battles. Which makes you wonder right away about the true function of the Coliseum, which may have nothing at all to do with gladiators or fighting at all, but may have been a structure that used the giant lake beneath it that never went away.

The Domus Aurea was said to be lost to history, buried under the Baths of Trajan until the 1400's when a young boy fell through a hole in the Esquiline hillside.[91] He found what seemed to be an old cave with beautiful painted walls. On hearing this, the artists of Rome began to also go down to the cave, soon to realize it was not a cave, but the lost Domus Aurea of Nero. While today these frescoes have started to fade on the plaster walls, at the time of their discovery they were still fresh. So new and unique were the paintings that when news of the find

---

[91]This falling through a hole story is very similar to the tale of a young boy falling through a hole to discover a great treasure near Rennes Le Chateau in the 1500's.

reached Florence (undergoing the Renaissance), Pinturicchio, Raphael and Michelangelo all made the trip to visit. Each carved their names on the walls to let the world know they had been there, as the paintings were a revelation of the true world of antiquity. Other tourist graffiti includes Casanova, the Marquis de Sade, Domenico Ghirlandaio, Martin van Heemskerck, and Filipino Lippi. I wonder if in fact these great artists would indeed carve their names into the walls of such a "special artistic find," thus defacing it. I am more likely the names were added later to create the story of the Renaissance.

The historical story claims that the find of the frescoes in the Domus Aurea were the direct cause of great changes that were started by Renaissance artists in the late 1400's (such as Raphael's decoration for the loggias in the Vatican). But is this true? Perhaps historians at a much later time (say the Domus Aurea was not really rediscovered until the 17 or 1800's) and as such needed a way to explain why the new found paintings in the Domus Aurea supposedly from AD 60 could look the same as the styles of the Renaissance that evolved in 1480 AD. Hence a story of the boy falling in and finding the site was created, along with the great masters coming to see being inspired by it to do the same. Everyone has since believed that story. Or maybe the Domus Aurea and the Renaissance in Florence were contemporary. They were not separated by 1500 years, but were being created at exactly the same time- which then would explain the similarity of the styles in the two places. Take a close look at the cover of this book again. Statue in a toga, giant dome like any of Rome's hundreds of churches, all in a layout like that of the Domus Aurea. It was a template for the US Fairs starting in Chicago- where each has the white buildings, domes and lakes that are a near copy of this Roman palace. Why are they copying it? It either has something to do with the original purpose of the Domus Aurea, which today we do not seem to understand. Or it had only recently been found (say 1850's and 60's) and the new exploration and what was found there was in turn mirrored in the expositions.

Statue of George Washington, looking very Roman-like, Nantes Gallery. You can find more Roman like toga figures from Napoleon to Russian Tzars.

When we come back to the examination of the expositions in America, and in fact the cities themselves, there is no doubt they are mirroring Ancient Rome. A city like Washington is a copy, with The Capitol and its dome, Union Station (designed by our Chicago builder Burnham and openly stating he designed it to copy Roman buildings), Lincoln Memorial (that resembles the Parthenon), White House, the Obelisk, Jefferson Memorial and many more. A story that appeared on the website ghostsofDC claims that an early estate in the Washington area was named Rome (supposedly because the owner was fond of Italy). Soon after nearby Goose Creek had its name changed to Tiber Creek (the Tiber the main river that runs through Rome). The seat of government in Rome is on the Capitoline Hill, while the seat of government in the US is at Capitol Hill. Add with this the geometric street layouts and mathematical placements of buildings. The other US cities are like Washington to some degree, and likely were far more so in the past. That is what makes understanding America's roots so difficult.

This book has been but an attempt at looking at questions surrounding the period 1800-1920 by using the expositions of the time as a model. When you go and look at images of Rome reconstructed, Rome in its glory, the expositions of the 1800's are almost a perfect match. And one has to ask why. I think similar people built the sites in Rome, Athens, and ones in the Americas- during the same time period. At this point I can not prove it...just as historians can not prove that they were built as standard history says. Standard history on this time frame just has a 120 year head start on us.

So what happened to these expositions? Who were the builders? What type of material was used, and what kind of building technology? How is the native Indian culture related to the history of these exposition cities? More research will follow in these areas, but it reached a point where the first section could become this book. Perhaps my writing will inspire you too to join in researching to find the truth of our history, a truth that seems to have been rewritten during this same period of time. Who are we, were did we come from, how did we get here?

All I can say at the end of this book is not that I have yet to find a definitive answer...but it is clear that the standard story we have been fed is a lie. That much is certain. We may not have "the answer" but at least when we can drop the story we are currently weighed down under. But dropping any story is scary for the mind. Stories are the foundation of who we are, where we are, and where we cam from. To see a story as a lie means we no longer know who we are. That is generally too scary so people will tend to hold onto any story (true or not) to feel safe. If you want to find Truth, in any area, then safe can not be your key word. Doubt must be your key word, and a burning desire to no longer be a lie.

The Domus Aurea was supposedly found when a boy fell down a hole, Oz found when Dorothy followed the rabbit down a hole, what is going to be our passage to reveal the truth of our past, and thus also reveal where this current messed up present known to us all originated?

Happy researching, falling and landing! May a burning desire come into you to find what is True.

BIBLIOGRAPHY and SOURCES

GENERAL
America's Fair, John Findling 2002 Smithsonian Press

studylove.org/worldsfairs

CHICAGO EXPOSITION

Handy PM, *Plans and Diagrams of All Exhibit Buildings in the World Columbian Exhibition*, (WB Conkey Company Chicago 1893)
Bancroft, Hugh, The Book of the Fair 3 Volumes, (Bancroft Company 1895)
Richard J Murphy, *Authentic Visitors Guide to the Worlds Columbian Exhibition and Chicago*, (The Union News Company, NY 1892)
Rossiter Johnson Ed., *History of the Worlds Columbian Exhibition Held in Chicago*, (D Appleton and Co 1897)
Rand McNally Guide to the Fair, 1893

http://columbus.gl.iit.edu/
https://www.friedmanfineart.net/vintage-1893-columbia-exposition-worlds-fair-photographs/
https://chicagology.com/columbiaexpo/
https://dcc.newberry.org/collections/chicago-and-the-worlds-columbian-exposition
https://en.wikipedia.org/wiki/World's_Columbian_Exposition

BUFFALO EXPOSITION
Creighton, Margaret, *The Rise and Fall of the Rainbow City*
Goldman, Mark, *High Hopes: The Rise and Decline of Buffalo*
Peckinpaugh, Roger, McKinley, *Murder and the Pan American Exposition*
panam1901.org
https://buffaloah.com/h/panam/goldman/

ST. LOUIS EXPOSITION

Buel JW, *Louisiana And The Fair*, 1904

Halstead, Murat (the well known author) that is what is says on the cover, *Pictorial History of the Louisiana Purchase and the Worlds Fair at St Louis*, (Publishing Company 1904)
Official Guide To The Louisiana Purchase Exposition 1904
The Piker and Worlds Fair Guide 1904
Rau, William official photographer, *The Forrest City* 1904,
Ansichen von der Weltausstelling (a English book partilly translated to German)
Final Report of the Louisiana Purchase Exposition Commission

Atthefair.com

Stolenhistory.org (A recommended source of discussion on all areas of questionable history)

PHOTO CREDITS

The majority of the photos in this book all come from public domain sources, normally a part of Wikmedia Commons. I have kept all such "rights" tags for the photos and can be presented if contacted.

Most images from the Columbian Exposition are from the online source : The Project Gutenberg EBook of Official Views Of The World's Columbian Exposition – http://www.gutenberg.org/files/22847/22847-h/22847-Author: C. D. Arnold and H. D. Higinbotham

All post 1924 photos are either taken by the author, or also come from Wikimedia Commons.

Should a photo be found to not be in public domain, and the copyright holder contacts me, I will gladly take it out of any future editions of this work at that point.

CHAPT 2

17 Wikimedia Commons, Original caption: "The Electric Tower - The Electric Tower is the crowning feature of the Exposition. It typifies the power of the elements, and especially the mysterious force of electricity, hence is surmounted by the winged figure of the Goddess of Light by Herbert Adams. From the ground to the tip of the torch held by this figure is 411 feet. John Galen Howard is the architect."C. D. Arnold - C. D. Arnold, Official Views of Pan-American Exposition, scanned by Dave Pape
Scan by NYPL - https://digitalcollections.nypl.org/items/510d47e0-5ef0-a3d9-e040-e00a18064a99

crystal palace london
The Crystal Palace, general view from the Water Temple.. Philip Henry Delamotte (1821–1889) - Smithsonian Libraries. This work is in the public domain in its country of origin and other countries and areas where the copyright term is the author's life plus 100 years or fewer.

Interior of the Crystal Palace
J. McNeven - collections.vam.ac.uk
McNeven, J., The Foreign Department, viewed towards the transept, coloured lithograph, 1851, Ackermann (printer), V&A. The interior of the Crystal Palace in London during the Great Exhibition of 1851.
English: McNeven, J., The Foreign Department, viewed towards the transept, coloured lithograph, 1851, Ackermann (printer), V&A. The interior of the Crystal Palace in London during the Great Exhibition of 1851.
Date   1851
Source   collections.vam.ac.uk

ny crystal palace
New York Crystal Palace, Frontispiece to New York Crystal Palace: illustrated description of the building by Geo. Carstensen & Chs. Gildemeister, architects of the building ; with an oil-color exterior view, and six large plates containing plans, elevations, sections, and details, from the working drawings of the architects (New York: Riker, Thorne & co., 1854)
Karl Gildemeister (1820-1869) - New York Crystal Palace at beinecke.library.yale.edu. Permission details public domain (old)

Die Abbildung ist ein Druck mit auf Ölfarbe basierende Tinte von George Baxter (1804 - 1867), London, datiert 1 September 1853. Authentisch durch den Mann, der eine Baxter Reklame-Tafel trägt.
Date   1854
Source   New York Crystal Palace at beinecke.library.yale.edu
Author   Karl Gildemeister (1820-1869)

Philadelphia
Cartaz da Exposição Internacional da Filadélfia em 1876, Arquivo Nacional

Trans cont hotel
. Trans-Continental Hotel. Alternate Title: International Exhibition, Philadelphia, 1876. 24. Published: 1876. Coverage: 1860?-1920?. Source Imprint: 1860?-1920?. Digital item published 9-30-2005; updated 2-13-2009. 331 Trans-Continental Hotel, from Robert N. Dennis collection of stereoscopic views 2
Contributor: The Picture Art Collection / Alamy Stock Photo
Image ID: P3FT51

Title: Panorama of Philadelphia and centennial exhibition grounds Physical description: 1 print. Notes: Associated name on shelflist card: Bachmann.; This record contains unverified data from PGA shelflist card.
Popular Graphic Arts - Library of Congress Catalog: http://lccn.loc.gov/2003679946 Image download: https://cdn.loc.gov/service/pnp/pga/00100/00105v.jpg Original url: http://hdl.loc.gov/loc.pnp/pga.00105
Rights advisory: No known restrictions on publication.

Gran Hotel Internacional
Date   appeared in the press in 1888
Source   Josep L. Roig, Historia de Barcelona, Ed. Primera Plana S.A., Barcelona, 1995, ISBN 84-8130-039-X
Author   graphist or photographer: Unknown; architect: Lluís Domènech i Montaner (1850-1923)

English: Hotel Internacional, projected by Lluís Domènech i Montaner for the Universal Exhibition at Barcelona, 1888; demolished in 1890
Date   1889
Source   http://www.skyscrapercity.com/showthread.php?p=70647083

"Birds-eye view of Louisville from the river front and Southern Exposition, 1883" by William F. Clarke
W. F. Clarke, Cincinnati, M.P. Levyeau & Co - This map is available from the United States Library of Congress's Geography & Map Division under the digital ID g3954l.pm002370. This tag does not indicate the copyright status of the attached work. A normal copyright tag is still required. See Commons:Licensing for more information.

    - AACR2: 651/1 .
Call Number/Physical Location
    G3954.L7A3 1883 .C6
Repository
    Library of Congress Geography and Map Division Washington, D.C. 20540-4650 USA dcu
Digital Id
    http://hdl.loc.gov/loc.gmd/g3954l.pm002370
The maps in the Map Collections materials were either published prior to 1922, produced by the United States government, or both (see catalogue records that accompany each map for information regarding date of publication and source). The Library of Congress is providing access to these materials for educational and research purposes and is not aware of any U.S. copyright protection (see Title 17 of the United States Code) or any other restrictions in the Map Collection materials.
Credit Line: Library of Congress, Geography and Map Division.

Garden Palace at the Sydney International Exhibition (1879)
http://www.slv.vic.gov.au/pictoria/a/1/4/doc/a14735.shtml
Australian International Exhibition, Sydney, 1879-1880 at the Garden Palace.

CHAPTER 3
U.S. Courthouse, Chicago, Illinois
FJC. - FJC, http://www.fjc.gov/history/courthouses.nsf/lookup/IL-Chicago_1905_Ref.jpg/$file/IL-Chicago_1905_Ref.jpg
Permission detailsPublic Domain File:Chicago Federal Court, 1961.jpg Created: 1 January 1961

US General Services Administration - US General Services Administration
    Public Domain
    File:Chicago Federal Center.jpg
    Created: 2007-00-00

Location: 41° 52' 44? N, 87° 37' 48? W

1832
By Rufus Blanchard, from drawing by George Davis -
http://publications.newberry.org/frontiertoheartland/items/show/155, Public Domain

1853 PIC
By unattributed - [http://collections.lib.uwm.edu/cdm/singleitem/collection/agdm/id/5647/rec/48,
Public Domain,

English: The raising of the briggs house in 1857 ([1]) or 1866 ([2])
Date   1857 or 1866
Source   Chicago Historical Society ([3])
Public domain
          This media file is in the public domain in the United States.
BRIGGS HOUSE
The Briggs House—a brick hotel—raised, probably in 1866.[33] unknown.. Jonathanriley at English
Wikipedia. Later version(s) were uploaded by Emijrp at English Wikipedia. - Chicago Historical
Society ([3])

panorama 1858
u of chicicago pics of cith 1858
Permalink
https://digital.library.illinois.edu/items/e410c040-1a05-0134-1d6d-0050569601ca-1

BRIGGS house
wikimedia commons
English: The raising of the briggs house in 1857 ([1]) or 1866 ([2])
Date   1857 or 1866
Source   Chicago Historical Society ([3])

Jonathanriley at English Wikipedia.
Later version(s) were uploaded by Emijrp at English Wikipedia.
Public domain
          This media file is in the public domain in the United States.

Hesler Panorama
From 1858, found on chicagology.com and greatchicagofire.org

FIRES
By Currier and Ives - Chicago Historical Society (ICHi-23436), Public Domain,

from NY times
By Currier and Ives - Chicago Historical Society (ICHi-23436), Public Domain,

CHICAGO 1898
https://commons.wikimedia.org/wiki/File:1898_Bird
{{Information |Description=Bird's-eye-view of the business district of Chicago |Source=
{{Institution:Library of Congress}} |Date=1898 |Author=Poole Brothers. |Permission={{PD-US}}
other_versions={{LOC-image|id=pm001530}} }}

OLD CITY HALL
sent by Chicago historian to me

new city hall

Chicago City Hall circa 1913
Gerson Bros. Chicago - Postcard
Chicago City Hall postage stamped November 9, 1914 postcard (front)

old chicago univerity
The Old University of Chicago

burnham root
PIC

Almost all of the photos appear in the 1894 book Shepp's World's Fair Photographed, by James W Shepp, Globe Bible Publishing 1893, Another is Portfoilio of Photographs of the Worlds Fair, 1893. Majority of the photos originally taken by CD Arnold. And the book uploaded by Guttenburg.

Between manufac and elect
"View North, Between Manufactures and Electricity Buildings." Large photographic print from The White City (As It Was). Photographs by William Henry Jackson. World's Columbian Exposition. 1893. Digitial Identifier: GN90799d_JWH_009w World's Columbian Exposition Collection at The Field Museum
The Field Museum Library - Between Manufactures and Electricity Buildings

Choral Hall from Wooded Island. Large photographic print from The White City (As It Was), photographs by William Henry Jackson. World's Columbian Exposition 1893. Digitial Identifier: GN90799d_JWH_044w World's Columbian Exposition Collection at The Field Museum
The Field Museum Library

World's Columbian Exposition 1893, by Axel Westerlind Identifier: grandestcenturyi00nort (find matches) Title: Grandest century in the world's history; containing a full and graphic account of the marvelous achievements of one hundred years, including great battles and conquests; the rise and fall of nations; wonderful growth and progress of the United States ... etc., etc Year: 1900 (1900s) Authors: Northrop, Henry Davenport, 1836-1909 Subjects: Nineteenth century Publisher: Philadelphia, Pa., National publishing co Contributing Library: The Library of Congress Digitizing Sponsor: Sloan Foundation View Book Page: Book Viewer About This Book: Catalog Entry View

Wood Pilings from the book The Century Worlds Fair Book for Boys and Girls. Pg 2

Government Building and Wooded Island. Large photographic print from The White City (As It Was), photographs by William Henry Jackson. World's Columbian Exposition 1893. Digitial Identifier: GN90799d_JWH_019w World's Columbian Exposition Collection at The Field Museum

The Field Museum Library - Government Building and Wooded Island
Permission details
The Field Museum Library @ Flickr Commons

Manufactures Building, from Horticultural Hall. Large photographic print from The White City (As It Was), photographs by William Henry Jackson. World's Columbian Exposition 1893. Digitial Identifier: GN90799d_JWH_002w World's Columbian Exposition Collection at The Field Museum
The Field Museum Library - Manufactures Building
Permission details
The Field Museum Library @ Flickr Commons
View more
    No restrictionsview terms

hubert banc

215

Hubert Howe Bancroft (1832–1918), American historian and ethnologist. Namesake of the Bancroft Library, University of California, Berkeley, USA.
Bradley   &   Rulofson   -   http://content.cdlib.org/ark:/13030/tf7d5nb5sw?
layout=metadata&brand=calisphere

sf lithograph
View of the Procession in Celebration of the Admission of California, Oct. 29, 1850, Crossing the Plaza of San Francisco, lithograph by John Prendergast

John Prendergast - Bancroft Library, University of California, Berkeley

View of the Procession in Celebration of the Admission of California, Oct. 29th, 1850, Crossing the Plaza of San Francisco, lithograph by John Prendergast, published by Zakreski and Hartman, Bancroft Library, University of California, Berkeley
Public Domain
File:Procession at San Francisco in Celebration of the Admission of California.jpg
Created: 1 January 1850

This is an image of a place or building that is listed on the National Register of Historic Places in the United States of America. Its reference number is
Victorgrigas - Own work
CC BY-SA 3.0
File:Chicago Cultural Center and Chicago Public Library, Chicago June 30, 2012-42.jpg
Created: 30 June 2012

Preston Bradley Hall1
Joseph Reagle - Own work
CC BY-SA 4.0
File:11-1338-dome-library-chicago.jpg
Created: 11 August 2018

Portsmouth Square, 1851.
Unknown - Library of Congress CALL NUMBER: DAG no. 1331
Portsmouth Square near harbor in 1851 — San Francisco during the Gold Rush. Early daguerrotype. Signs in image include: California Restaurant, Book and Job Printing, Louisiana, Sociedad, Drugs & Medicines Wholesale & Retail, Henry Johnson & Co, Alta California, Bella Union, A. Holmes.
Permission details
Public Domainview terms
File:SanFrancisco1851a.jpg
Created: before June 22, 1851

HARBOUR 1851
Unknown - This image is available from the United States Library of Congress's Prints and Photographs division under the digital ID cph.3g07421. This tag does not indicate the copyright status of the attached work. A normal copyright tag is still required. See Commons:Licensing for more information.
San Francisco harbor at Yerba Buena Cove in 1850 or 1851 — with Yerba Buena Island, and Berkeley Hills, in the background. Daguerrotype, from during the California Gold Rush.
Public Domain
File:SanFranciscoharbor1851c sharp.jpg
Created: 1 January 1850

Poster of the Panama–Pacific International Exposition, held in San Francisco, US.
Unknown - San Francisco Public Library
  Public Domain
  File:Panama pacific poster.jpg
  Created: 1 January 1915

panorama
https://commons.wikimedia.org/wiki/File:Panorama_of_San_Francisco_by_Eadweard_Muybridge,_1878.jpg
This is a faithful photographic reproduction of a two-dimensional, public domain work of art. The work of art itself is in the public domain for the following reason: The author died in 1904, so this work is in the public domain in its country of origin and other countries and areas where the copyright term is the author's life plus 100 years or less.

TENN CALENDAR
Tennessee Centennial Exposition TeVA Collection, Tennessee State Library and Archives
Saraeileen89 - Own work
This promotional calendar from 1897 featured various buildings each month , including this colorful drawing of the Parthenon. Tennessee Centennial Exposition, Tennessee State Library and Archives.
  CC BY-SA 4.0
  File:Tennessee Centennial Promotional Calendar.jpg
  Created: 1 October 2018

This is an image of a place or building that is listed on the National Register of Historic Places in the United States of America. Its reference number is
Mayur Phadtare - Own work
  CC BY-SA 3.0
  File:Parthenon, Nashville.JPG
  Created: 15 September 2012

OMAHA
public domain,
original photos 1892 by RA Renehart

trans miss pics
orig photographer
F. A. Rinehart - Photographs by F. A. Rinehart

night illumination
Detroit Publishing Co. - This image is available from the United States Library of Congress's Prints and Photographs division under the digital ID ppmsca.18029. This tag does not indicate the copyright status of the attached work. A normal copyright tag is still required. See Commons:Licensing for more information.

BUFF
most are by CD Arnold
C. D. Arnold - C. D. Arnold, Official Views of Pan-American Exposition, scanned by Dave Pape

Ethnology and Government Buildings
C. D. Arnold - C. D. Arnold, Official Views of Pan-American Exposition, scanned by Dave Pape

217

Original caption: "Ethnology and Government Buildings - The Ethnology Building is classic in outline with Renaissance decorative treatment. While it corresponds in form with the Temple of Music, across the Court of Fountains, it has a distinct character of its own. The building has a dome resembling that of the Pantheon at Rome. The architect is Mr. George Cary."
Public Domainview terms
File:Pan-American Exposition - Ethnology and Government Buildings.jpg
Created: 1 January 1901

Electric tower photo
Original caption: "The Electric Tower - The Electric Tower is the crowning feature of the Exposition. It typifies the power of the elements, and especially the mysterious force of electricity, hence is surmounted by the winged figure of the Goddess of Light by Herbert Adams. From the ground to the tip of the torch held by this figure is 411 feet. John Galen Howard is the architect."
Date   1901
Source   C. D. Arnold, Official Views of Pan-American Exposition, scanned by Dave Pape
Author   C. D. Arnold

panorama
unidentified photographer, from "The Latest and Best Views of the Pan-American Exposition", Buffalo,   N.Y.:   Robert   Allen   Reid,   1901   -   University   of   Buffalo: http://ublib.buffalo.edu/libraries/exhibits/panam/art/architecture/panorama.html

Pan-American Exhibition, Buffalo, New York, 1901, panorama view
Permission details
Public domain
View more
Public Domainview terms
File:Pan-American Exhibition 1901 Panorama.jpg
Created: 1 January 1901

McKinley arrives at the Temple of Music, shortly before being shot.
E. Benjamin Andrews - Andrews, E. Benjamin. History of the United States, volume V. Charles Scribner's Sons, New York. 1912, p. 363
One of the last photographs of the late President McKinley. Taken as he was ascending the steps of the Temple of Music, September 6, 1901.
Public Domain
File:McKinley last photo.jpg
Created: 6 September 1901

Logo of the Pan-American Exposition
Raphael Beck - http://www.nps.gov/archive/thri/PanAmExhibit.htm
Permission details
Public domain image from National Park Service website

Grand coutromaha
Night view of the Grand Court. Photograph by Frank Rinehart, 1898.
Description: At the Trans-Mississippi and International Exposition, Omaha, Nebraska a view of the Grand Court with a collection of large, white fair buildings arranged around a large reflecting pool. The Smithsonian coordinated all of the U.S. Government exhibits and prepared a display on its activities and collections for the exposition. Creator/Photographer: Unidentified photographer Medium: Cyanotype Dimensions: 8 in x 10 in Date: 1898 Repository: Smithsonian Institution Archives Accession number: 12782

Smithsonian Institution from United States-- Trans-Mississippi Expo, Grand Court, Omaha
Permission details
Smithsonian Institution @ Flickr Common

fountain
"Fountain of Neptune", Trans-Mississippi Exposition, Omaha, Nebraska, 1898
Frank A. Rinehart - 1898 photo by F. A. Rinehart via [1]
Permission details
Copyright 1898 by F.A. Rinhart; copyright expired

trans miss photos can all be found at
http://trans-mississippi.unl.edu/photographs/bluff_tract.html

stl couthouse
The old St. Louis County courthouse in downtown St.Louis, Missouri, commonly known as the Old Courthouse.
Raymond F. Adams - http://collections.mohistory.org/resource/140771.html

govt bld
"Neoclassical architecture in the Government Building at the Louisiana Purchase Exposition" (aka St. Louis World's Fair, 1904)
David R. Francis (book author) - The Universal Exposition of 1904 (St. Louis: Louisiana Purchase Exposition Company, 1905), p. 91
Permission details
Public domain
View more
  Public Domainview terms
  File:Louisiana Purchase Exposition St. Louis 1904.jpg
  Created: 1904, published 1905

fest hall
Title: "Acme of Splendor, Hydrangea Beds, Festival Hall and Cascades, Louisiana Purchase Exposition, St. Louis, MO, U.S.A."
Keystone View Company - Missouri History Museum URL: http://images.mohistory.org/image/FC4F0574-BAE9-0106-2A51-5F5E724D5A7D/original.jpg
Gallery: http://collections.mohistory.org/resource/142223
Permission details
UND - Copyright undetermined MHS Open Access Policy: You are welcome to download and utilize any digital file that the Missouri Historical believes is likely in the public domain or is free of other known restrictions. This content is available free of charge and may be used without seeking permission from the Missouri Historical Society.
View more
  Public Domainview terms

Boer cavl
Title: "Boer Cavalry ready for Mimic War." Boer War Exhibit at the 1904 World's Fair.

Official Photographic Company - Missouri History Museum URL: http://images.mohistory.org/image/9E7452BB-4B71-9B59-901F-981188007125/original.jpg Gallery: http://collections.mohistory.org/resource/148743
Permission details
UND - Copyright undetermined MHS Open Access Policy: You are welcome to download and utilize any digital file that the Missouri Historical believes is likely in the public domain or is free of other

known restrictions. This content is available free of charge and may be used without seekin
permission from the Missouri Historical Society.
View more
    Public Domainview terms
    File:"Boer Cavalry ready for Mimic War." Boer War Exhibit at the 1904 World's Fair.jpg
    Created: 1 January 1904

cannibal
Title: "Cannibal." (Ota Benga, Pygmy. Part of Department of Anthropology at the 1904 World's Fair

Gerhard Sisters - Missouri History Museum URL: http://images.mohistory.org/image/565A0C5(
F9AC-837C-2158-E962925AB687//original.jpg   Galler
http://collections.mohistory.org/resource/147383
Permission details
UND - Copyright undetermined MHS Open Access Policy: You are welcome to download and utiliz
any digital file that the Missouri Historical believes is likely in the public domain or is free of othe
known restrictions. This content is available free of charge and may be used without seekin
permission from the Missouri Historical Society.
View more
    Public Domainview terms
    File:"Cannibal." (Ota Benga, Pygmy. Part of Department of Anthropology at the 1904 World
Fair).jpg
    Created: 1 January 1904

secnd geron
Title: "Chief Geronimo." (NOTE: Not the Apache Geronimo). Department of Anthropology, 190
World's Fair.

Jessie   Tarbox   Beals   (attributed)   -   Missouri   History   Museum   URI
http://images.mohistory.org/image/B4382DF8-E528-70F4-7506-DCA57584FA39/original.jpg
Gallery: http://collections.mohistory.org/resource/149408
Permission details
UND - Copyright undetermined MHS Open Access Policy: You are welcome to download and utiliz
any digital file that the Missouri Historical believes is likely in the public domain or is free of othe
known restrictions. This content is available free of charge and may be used without seekin
permission from the Missouri Historical Society.
View more
    Public Domainview terms
    File:"Chief Geronimo." (NOTE- Not the Apache Geronimo). Department of Anthropology, 190
World's Fair.jpg
    Created: 1 January 1904

looking over to manauf build
Title: "From tower of Electricity Building, northeast over Basin and Plaza to Manufactures Building
World's Fair, St. Louis, USA." [Louisiana Purchase Exposition]. U and U 48.
Underwood   and   Underwood   -   Missouri   History   Museum   URL
http://images.mohistory.org/image/D6F369C7-B039-13DF-73D7-E8D116C80929/original.jpg
Gallery: http://collections.mohistory.org/resource/145119
Permission details
UND - Copyright undetermined MHS Open Access Policy: You are welcome to download and utiliz
any digital file that the Missouri Historical believes is likely in the public domain or is free of othe
known restrictions. This content is available free of charge and may be used without seekin
permission from the Missouri Historical Society.
View more
    Public Domainview terms
    File:"From tower of Electricity Building, northeast over Basin and Plaza to Manufactures Building
World's Fair, St. Louis, USA." (Louisiana Purchase Exposition). U and U 48.jpg

Created: 1 January 1904

sign great achiev
Title: "From tower of Electricity Building, northeast over Basin and Plaza to Manufactures Building, World's Fair, St. Louis, USA." [Louisiana Purchase Exposition]. U and U 48.

Underwood and Underwood - Missouri History Museum URL: http://images.mohistory.org/image/D6F369C7-B039-13DF-73D7-E8D116C80929/original.jpg
Gallery: http://collections.mohistory.org/resource/145119
Permission details
UND - Copyright undetermined MHS Open Access Policy: You are welcome to download and utilize any digital file that the Missouri Historical believes is likely in the public domain or is free of other known restrictions. This content is available free of charge and may be used without seeking permission from the Missouri Historical Society.
View more
  Public Domainview terms
  File:"From tower of Electricity Building, northeast over Basin and Plaza to Manufactures Building, World's Fair, St. Louis, USA." (Louisiana Purchase Exposition). U and U 48.jpg
  Created: 1 January 1904

agri
Title: "Palace of Agriculture and Floral Clock." View south past Ceylon and Canada Buildings at the 1904 World's Fair.
Official Photographic Company - Missouri History Museum URL: http://images.mohistory.org/image/F9B6CC64-02EB-2188-AB21-800EB5E244A4/original.jpg
Gallery: http://collections.mohistory.org/resource/146951
Permission details
UND - Copyright undetermined MHS Open Access Policy: You are welcome to download and utilize any digital file that the Missouri Historical believes is likely in the public domain or is free of other known restrictions. This content is available free of charge and may be used without seeking permission from the Missouri Historical Society.

pawnee
800px-'Pawnee_Indian.'_Department_of_Anthropology,_1904_World's_Fair

seville bld
Title: "Sevilla Building." Streets of Seville attraction on the Pike at the 1904 World's Fair.

Unknown - Missouri History Museum URL: http://images.mohistory.org/image/A6E48C50-72DE-8948-A93E-8AE2AC74D068/original.jpg Gallery: http://collections.mohistory.org/resource/148734
Permission details
UND -

bathe infant
Title: "Sevilla Building." Streets of Seville attraction on the Pike at the 1904 World's Fair.

Unknown - Missouri History Museum URL: http://images.mohistory.org/image/A6E48C50-72DE-8948-A93E-8AE2AC74D068/original.jpg Gallery: http://collections.mohistory.org/resource/148734
Permission details
UND -

pretty birch drive
Title: "The Pretty Birch Drive." (View of Forest Park prior to construction for the 1904 World's Fair).
George Stark - Missouri History Museum URL: http://images.mohistory.org/image/5AD6CB22-8D9A-09F1-39BC-D743AAAF7ED2/original.jpg   Gallery: http://collections.mohistory.org/resource/145099
Permission details

UND -

zenith of beauty
Title: "The Zenith of Beauty, Art Hill, Louisiana Purchase Exposition, St. Louis, MO., U.S.A."

Keystone View Company - Missouri History Museum URL:
http://images.mohistory.org/image/35729307-21A0-A491-92B8-20783D332B86/original.jpg Gallery:
http://collections.mohistory.org/resource/142281
Permission details
UND -

admin bldg
Title: 1904 World's Fair Administration Building (Brookings Hall, Washington University) seen from
the southeast with the Italian Pavilion in the foreground.

Official Photographic Company - Missouri History Museum URL:
http://images.mohistory.org/image/C7E2403C-B299-5CF9-DEBC-457EE08126B1/original.jpg
Gallery: http://collections.mohistory.org/resource/141502
Permission details
UND - Copyright undetermined MHS Open Access Policy: You are welcome to download and utilize
any digital file that the Missouri Historical believes is likely in the public domain or is free of other
known restrictions. This content is available free of charge and may be used without seeking
permission from the Missouri Historical Society.
View more
    Public Domainview terms
    File:1904 World's Fair Administration Building (Brookings Hall, Washington University) seen from
the southeast with the Italian Pavilion in the foreground.jpg
    Created

process on pike
Title: A procession forming up on the Pike on Pike Day at the 1904 World's Fair.
Official Photographic Company - Missouri History Museum URL:
http://images.mohistory.org/image/48CCE8E9-1B03-F0FA-FB35-96EA4FCBA54E/original.jpg
Gallery: http://collections.mohistory.org/resource/141430
Permission details
UND - Copyright undetermined MHS Open Access Policy: You are welcome to download and utilize
any digital file that the Missouri Historical believes is likely in the public domain or is free of other
known restrictions. This content is available free of charge and may be used without seeking
permission from the Missouri Historical Society.
View more

    Public Domainview terms
    File:A procession forming up on the Pike on Pike Day at the 1904 World's Fair.jpg
    Created: 1 January 1904

ARIEL VIEW FRMO DEF TOEWR
Title: Aerial view from the DeForest Wireless Tower looking over the 1904 World's Fair grounds
towards Festival Hall.
F.J. Koster - Missouri History Museum URL: http://images.mohistory.org/image/5A160064-CD0E-
07D3-81BC-3EBABB8DDBA7/original.jpg Gallery: http://collections.mohistory.org/resource/141472
Permission details
UND - Copyright undetermined MHS Open Access Policy: You are welcome to download and utilize
any digital file that the Missouri Historical believes is likely in the public domain or is free of other
known restrictions. This content is available free of charge and may be used without seeking
permission from the Missouri Historical Society.

View more

File:Aerial view from the DeForest Wireless Tower looking over the 1904 World's Fair grounds towards Festival Hall.jpg
Created: 1 January 1904

About this interface | Discussion | Help

TRYOLEAN
Title: Arm wrestling of the Tyroleans, the Town Hall at the Tyrolean Alps on the Pike at the 1904 World's Fair.
Unknown - Missouri History Museum URL: http://images.mohistory.org/image/727F93AE-6A3C-194A-1224-AD4A5644D931/original.jpg Gallery: http://collections.mohistory.org/resource/141516
Permission details
View more

File:Arm wrestling of the Tyroleans, the Town Hall at the Tyrolean Alps on the Pike at the 1904 World's Fair.jpg
Created: 1 January 1904

PALC OF AGRI INTERI
Title: Birdseye view of the interior of the Palace of Agriculture at the 1904 World's Fair showing Whitman Agricultural Company exhibit in the foreground.
Official Photographic Company - Missouri History Museum URL: http://images.mohistory.org/image/FAECEF2F-B5B8-DC0F-2594-953E236051ED/original.jpg
Gallery: http://collections.mohistory.org/resource/146107
Permission details
View more

MNF
Title: Birdseye view of the Palace of Manufactures from the DeForest Wireless Tower at the 1904 World's Fair.
F.J. Koster - Missouri History Museum URL: http://images.mohistory.org/image/8880F4FE-C630-139E-0C09-164E52C748C9/original.jpg Gallery: http://collections.mohistory.org/resource/146722
Permission details
View more
File:

CARP 10 JUNE 1902

223

Title: Carpenters drilling holes and placing bolts in timbers during construction for the 1904 World's Fair, 10 June 1902.

George Stark - Missouri History Museum URL: http://images.mohistory.org/image/69BC5875-9102-73B5-1653-E4EE59787D1F/original.jpg Gallery: http://collections.mohistory.org/resource/145612
Permission details
UND - Copyright undetermined MHS Open Access Policy: You are welcome to download and utilize any digital file that the Missouri Historical believes is likely in the public domain or is free of other known restrictions. This content is available free of charge and may be used without seeking permission from the Missouri Historical Society.
View more
Public Domainview terms
File:Carpenters drilling holes and placing bolts in timbers during construction for the 1904 World's Fair, 10 June 1902.jpg
Created: 10 June 1902

CONSTRCT STDM
Title: Construction of stadium built for the 1904 Olympics, 9 January 1904.
Unknown - Missouri History Museum URL: http://images.mohistory.org/image/93C89AAA-A7E8-90FB-DA52-96C801F55FAF/original.jpg Gallery: http://collections.mohistory.org/resource/142446
Permission details
UND - Copyright undetermined MHS Open Access Policy: You are welcome to download and utilize any digital file that the Missouri Historical believes is likely in the public domain or is free of other known restrictions. This content is available free of charge and may be used without seeking permission from the Missouri Historical Society.
View more
Public Domainview terms
File:Construction of stadium built for the 1904 Olympics, 9 January 1904.jpg
Created: 9 January 1904

CONSTT WATER CHANEL
Title: Construction on the channel way for the River Des Peres in Forest Park in preparation for the 1904 World's Fair.
George Stark - Missouri History Museum URL: http://images.mohistory.org/image/5ADCD78A-6AA7-E8BC-0727-5C3642DC56D8/original.jpg   Gallery: http://collections.mohistory.org/resource/141311
Permission details
UND - Copyright undetermined MHS Open Access Policy: You are welcome to download and utilize any digital file that the Missouri Historical believes is likely in the public domain or is free of other known restrictions. This content is available free of charge and may be used without seeking permission from the Missouri Historical Society.

HORSES BULLING STUMSPS
Title: Draft horse pulling a stump during the excavation for the River des Peres in Forest Park during the construction phase of the 1904 World's Fair, 15 February 1902.
George Stark - Missouri History Museum URL: http://images.mohistory.org/image/2D1CF0EA-E765-0901-617B-FAF416B7504E/original.jpg   Gallery: http://collections.mohistory.org/resource/141463
Permission details
UND - Copyright undetermined MHS Open Access Policy: You are welcome to download and utilize any digital file that the Missouri Historical believes is likely in the public domain or is free of other known restrictions. This content is available free of charge and may be used without seeking permission from the Missouri Historical Society.
View more
Public Domainview terms

File:Draft horse pulling a stump during the excavation for the River des Peres in Forest Park during the construction phase of the 1904 World's Fair, 15 February 1902.jpg
Created

ENT PALAE OF ED
Title: Entrance to the Palace of Education across the Grand Basin at the 1904 World's Fair.
Official Photographic Company - Missouri History Museum URL: http://images.mohistory.org/image/4A0AA8B9-C2D4-B6D4-677C-ED95A1E0C437/original.jpg
Gallery: http://collections.mohistory.org/resource/141506
Permission details
UND - Copyright undetermined MHS Open Access Policy: You are welcome to download and utilize any digital file that the Missouri Historical believes is likely in the public domain or is free of other known restrictions. This content is available free of charge and may be used without seeking permission from the Missouri Historical Society.
View more

Public Domainview terms
File:Entrance to the Palace of Education across the Grand Basin at the 1904 World's Fair.jpg
Created: 1 January 1904

About this interface | Discussion | Help

FEST HALL W CASCADES
Title: Festival Hall with the Central Cascade fountain in operation at the 1904 World's Fair.
Official Photographic Company - Missouri History Museum URL: http://images.mohistory.org/image/41AA5501-122B-94BF-21D2-6BC2505BC4FD/original.jpg
Gallery: http://collections.mohistory.org/resource/145937
Permission details
UND - Copyright undetermined MHS Open Access Policy: You are welcome to download and utilize any digital file that the Missouri Historical believes is likely in the public domain or is free of other known restrictions. This content is available free of charge and may be used without seeking permission from the Missouri Historical Society.
View more
Public Domainview terms
File:Festival Hall with the Central Cascade fountain in operation at the 1904 World's Fair.jpg
Created: 1 January 1904

FEST HALL W CASCADESE 2 WIDER SHOT
Title: Festival Hall, Cascades and Lagoon at the 1904 World's Fair seen from the northwest.
Emil Boehl - Missouri History Museum URL: http://images.mohistory.org/image/65A5B6AC-FAAC-45A4-33BA-3122789E275A/original.jpg Gallery: http://collections.mohistory.org/resource/141467
Permission details
UND - Copyright undetermined MHS Open Access Policy: You are welcome to download and utilize any digital file that the Missouri Historical believes is likely in the public domain or is free of other known restrictions. This content is available free of charge and may be used without seeking permission from the Missouri Historical Society.
View more
Public Domainview terms
File:Festival Hall, Cascades and Lagoon at the 1904 World's Fair seen from the northwest.jpg
Created: 1 January 1904

FELID OF STUMPS W ADMIN IN DISATNCE
VERY VERY IMPORATNT PHOTO FROM 1902

225

Title: Field of stumps with the Administration Building in distance during construction phase of the 1904 World's Fair.
George Stark - Missouri History Museum URL: http://images.mohistory.org/image/F5C6C501-82FC 6C02-635E-88764B4F87DD/original.jpg Gallery: http://collections.mohistory.org/resource/141464
Permission details
UND - Copyright undetermined MHS Open Access Policy: You are welcome to download and utilize any digital file that the Missouri Historical believes is likely in the public domain or is free of other known restrictions. This content is available free of charge and may be used without seeking permission from the Missouri Historical Society.
View more
  Public Domainview terms
  File:Field of stumps with the Administration Building in distance during construction phase of the 1904 World's Fair.jpg
  Created: 1 January 1902

NIGHT VIEW OF FEST HALL'
Title: Night view of Festival Hall and the Central Cascades at the 1904 World's Fair.
Official   Photographic   Company   -   Missouri   History   Museum   URL
http://images.mohistory.org/image/A06B41D3-6811-2519-F933-D45D3A57C288/original.jpg
Gallery: http://collections.mohistory.org/resource/146202
Permission details
UND - Copyright undetermined MHS Open Access Policy: You are welcome to download and utilize any digital file that the Missouri Historical believes is likely in the public domain or is free of other known restrictions. This content is available free of charge and may be used without seeking permission from the Missouri Historical Society.
View more
  Public Domainview terms
  File:Night view of Festival Hall and the Central Cascades at the 1904 World's Fair.jpg
  Created: 1 January 1904

PALACE OF ART
Title: Palace of Art at the 1904 World's Fair.
Unknown - Missouri History Museum URL: http://images.mohistory.org/image/7C09FA4C-B7C9 C6BE-1500-EB2FEB84E023/original.jpg Gallery: http://collections.mohistory.org/resource/141335
Permission details
UND - Copyright undetermined MHS Open Access Policy: You are welcome to download and utilize any digital file that the Missouri Historical believes is likely in the public domain or is free of other known restrictions. This content is available free of charge and may be used without seeking permission from the Missouri Historical Society.
View more
  Public Domainview terms
  File:Palace of Art at the 1904 World's Fair.jpg
  Created: 1 January 1904

BOEER WAR REINACT
Title: Re-enactment of a Boer War battle scene on the Pike at the 1904 World's Fair.
Official   Photographic   Company   -   Missouri   History   Museum   URL
http://images.mohistory.org/image/A8195E09-AEA1-6239-F7AF-58F09AE0FECF/original.jpg
Gallery: http://collections.mohistory.org/resource/146273
Permission details
UND - Copyright undetermined MHS Open Access Policy: You are welcome to download and utilize any digital file that the Missouri Historical believes is likely in the public domain or is free of other known restrictions. This content is available free of charge and may be used without seeking permission from the Missouri Historical Society.
View more

File:Re-enactment of a Boer War battle scene on the Pike at the 1904 World's Fair.jpg
Created: 1 January 1904

US GOT BLD LONG VIEW
Title: U.S. Government Building at the 1904 World's Fair.
Official Photographic Company - Missouri History Museum URL: http://images.mohistory.org/image/974161A6-192D-D2F2-B397-9165A5965E82/original.jpg Gallery: http://collections.mohistory.org/resource/142019
Permission details
File:U.S. Government Building at the 1904 World's Fair.jpg
Created: 1 January 1904

CONSTRUCT PALACE OF ART
Title: View of construction on the Palace of Art looking from the north east at the 1904 World's Fair site, September 1903.
Official Photographic Company (Byrnes) - Missouri History Museum URL: http://images.mohistory.org/image/E11CBD4C-7C3B-C851-4B91-2EB95A38FFC8/original.jpg Gallery: http://collections.mohistory.org/resource/148508
Permission details

GERON
Apache chief Geronimo, photographed at the St. Louis World's Fair in 1904 by William H. Rau. This image has been cropped from a stereo card found here.

William H. Rau (1855–1920) - This image is available from the United States Library of Congress's Prints and Photographs division under the digital ID cph.3c07536. This tag does not indicate the copyright status of the attached work. A normal copyright tag is still required. See Commons:Licensing for more information.
File:Wrau-geronimo-1904-worlds-fair-cropped.jpg
Created: 1 January 1904

ROOFING
Title: Workers roofing the Electricity Building during the construction phase of the 1904 World's Fair.
Byrnes Photographic Company - Missouri History Museum URL: http://images.mohistory.org/image/089883D6-A2CD-E0CA-FA25-288B0A4D7A96/original.jpg Gallery: http://collections.mohistory.org/resource/141350
Permission details
File:Workers roofing the Electricity Building during the construction phase of the 1904 World's Fair.jpg

Created: 1 January 1903

WORKERS HOIST STAFF
Title: Workers hoisting staff onto the Palace of Varied Industries building during construction for the 1904 World's Fair.
George Stark - Missouri History Museum URL: http://images.mohistory.org/image/3DAE5231-8A50-E8FF-CEFD-2B790FE34FD6/original.jpg Gallery: http://collections.mohistory.org/resource/141461
Permission details
UND - Copyright undetermined MHS Open Access Policy: You are welcome to download and utilize any digital file that the Missouri Historical believes is likely in the public domain or is free of other known restrictions. This content is available free of charge and may be used without seeking permission from the Missouri Historical Society.
View more
    Public Domainview terms
    File:Workers hoisting staff onto the Palace of Varied Industries building during construction for the 1904 World's Fair.jpg
    Created: 1 January 1902

SUNKEN GARDEN
Title: View of the Sunken Gardens with the Palace of Liberal Arts (left), U.S. Government Building (center), and the Palace of Mines and Metallurgy (right) at the 1904 World's Fair.
Official   Photographic   Company   -   Missouri   History   Museum   URL: http://images.mohistory.org/image/63B03B15-6C29-8608-811E-8737CF369B29/original.jpg Gallery: http://collections.mohistory.org/resource/146361
Permission details
UND - Copyright undetermined MHS Open Access Policy: You are welcome to download and utilize any digital file that the Missouri Historical believes is likely in the public domain or is free of other known restrictions. This content is available free of charge and may be used without seeking permission from the Missouri Historical Society.
View more

    Public Domainview terms
    File:View of the Sunken Gardens with the Palace of Liberal Arts (left), U.S. Government Building (center), and the Palace of Mines and Metallurgy (right) at the 1904 World's Fair.jpg
    Created: 1 January 1904

    Public Domain
    File:Tennessee Centennial Exposition 1897 (LOC ppmsca.03354).jpg
        Created: circa 1896 date QS:P571,+1896-00-00T00:00:00Z/9,P1480,Q5727902. SUBJECTS Tennessee Centennial and International Exposition--(1897 :--Nashville, Tenn.) Exhibitions--Tennessee--Nashville--1890-1900.   Centennial   celebrations--Tennessee--Nashville--1890-1900. FORMAT Bird's-eye view prints

Original work:File:Zinc anode 2.png by User:MichelJullian (talk) Derivative work: KES47 (talk) - File:Copper cathode 2.png

cht 8

Magnetron schematic section
View author information
    CC BY-SA 3.0
    File:Magnetron schematic section.jpg
    Uploaded: 14 April 2005

cathode
English: Copper cathode.
Date 21 October 2010
Source File:Copper cathode 2.png
Author
Original work:File:Zinc anode 2.png by User:MichelJullian (talk)
Derivative work: KES47 (talk)

Inkscape-un.svg
This W3C-unspecified vector image was created with Inkscape.
Licensing
GNU head Permission is granted to copy, distribute and/or modify this document under the terms of the GNU Free Documentation License, Version 1.2 or any later version published by the Free Software Foundation; with no Invariant Sections, no Front-Cover Texts, and no Back-Cover Texts. A copy of the license is included in the section entitled GNU Free Documentation License.
w:en:Creative Commons
attribution share alike This file is licensed under the Creative Commons Attribution-Share Alike 3.0 Unported license.

palmanova
Italiano: Panorama satellite
Date 27 March 2019
Source Own work
Author A.D.L
Licensing
I, the copyright holder of this work, hereby publish it under the following license:
w:en:Creative Commons

This file is licensed under the Creative Commons Attribution-Share Alike 4.0 International license.

You are free:
to share – to copy, distribute and transmit the work
to remix – to adapt the work

baltimore fire
Published/Created [1904]
digital file from original http://hdl.loc.gov/loc.pnp/npcc.18732
https://lccn.loc.gov/2016844571
Rights advisory
No known restrictions on publication. For more information, see National Photo Company Collection - Rights and Restrictions Information https://www.loc.gov/rr/print/res/275_npco.html

Boston fire 2
Boston, after the fire, November 9th & 10th, 1872. Digitally enhanced (colors adjusted & tear partially hidden) by Dave Pape.
Date 1872
Source Library of Congress Prints and Photographs Division. http://hdl.loc.gov/loc.pnp/pan.6a06305
Author Smith, Joshua, copyright claimant
Permission
(Reusing this file)
Original photo is public domain (U.S. pre-1923). Modified version released to public domain by Dave Pape.

Portland maine
  by John P. Soule.
Title   Looking down Middle St., from Rich's Printing Office, showing portion of Temple and
Exchange Sts., and U.S. Custom House.
Alternative title   Ruins of the Great Fire in Portland, Me., July 4, 1866. 471.
Date   1866
Source   https://digitalcollections.nypl.org/items/510d47e0-27d6-a3d9-e040-e00a18064a99
Author   Scan by NYPL
Free to use without restriction

chicago fire
 ICHi-002811Headline: Corner of State and Madison Streets after the Chicago Fire of 1871 Date
Depicted: 1871 Creator: Unknown Artwork/Object Depicted: photographic prints Copyright Notice:
No known copyright restrictions. Credit Line: Chicago History Museum, ICHi-002811

Napoleon statue
Deutsch: Pariser Kommune 1871 beim Sturz der Colonne Vendôme
English: Destruction of the Vendôme Colonne during the Paris Commune.
Français : La colonne Vendôme renversée durant la Commune de Paris.
Date   May 1871
Source   http://www.republique.ch/archives/enavant/mai98/insurrection.html
Author   André Adolphe Eugène Disdéri (1819 - 1889)
Other versions

ABOUT THE AUTHOR

Howard Mickoski is the author of several books on history and spiritual wisdom.

Those wishing to support his research, offer assistance or share what they have been studying can reach him through his website

egyptian-wisdom-revealed.com

or his email

egypthowdie@outlook.com

OTHER BOOKS BY AUTHOR:
FALLING FOR TRUTH-A Spiritual Death and Awakening
THE POWER OF THEN-Revealing Egypt's Lost Wisdom
TWELVE MONTHS OF MYSTICAL WISDOM
HOCKEYOLOGY

New research available in 2020 on the Knights Templar, Cathars and the Holy Grail. Stay tuned.

Families **Together** in Albany County

in Partnership with Albany County Department for Children, Youth & Families

WM

DOMES
CLOCK TOWERS
CASTLES
columns
STEEPLES

Albany Family Center • P: 518.432.0333 • 737 Madison Ave. • Albany, NY 12208 • F: 518.434.6478 **Colonie**

• F: 518.218.1051 **Hilltows Family Center** • P: 518.872.1460 • 96 Main St. • East Berne, NY 12059 • F: 518.872.1465

Family Center • P: 518.218.1030 • 1639 Central Ave. • Colonie, NY 12205

233

Thanks for reading!

CPSIA information can be obtained
at www.ICGtesting.com
Printed in the USA
LVHW050035201220
674642LV00004B/442